DAVID WEATHERLY

BEEHIVE STATE MONSTERS

CRYPTIDS & LEGENDS
OF
UTAH
FOREWORD BY DAVID J. WEST

Eerie Lights Publishing
Eerielightspublishing.com

DAVID WEATHERLY
BEEHIVE STATE MONSTERS
CRYPTIDS & LEGENDS
OF
UTAH
FOREWORD BY DAVID J. WEST
Based on interviews and research conducted by David Weatherly

ISBN: 978-1-945950-35-3 (Paperback)

Published by:

EERIE LIGHTS

Eerie Lights Publishing
Eerielightspublishing.com

Cover design: Sam Shearon
www.mister-sam.com

Editor: Jerry Hajewski

Book layout/design: SMAK
www.smakgraphics.com

Printed in the United States of America

Also by David Weatherly

Table of Contents

Foreword

This is the Place for the strange.

I have spent about half of my life in Utah, and yet David Weatherly was able to track down a whole lot of stories I had not heard yet. Color me impressed.

I write action-adventure pulp fiction with quite a bit of supernatural flavoring mixed in and love finding out about anything weird anywhere I can. Like anyone who is picking up this book, I have loved reading about Bigfoot and the Loch Ness monster since I was a kid, and as I got older, that healthy wonderment increased until I had to admit that the trickster is hard at work here. I've had pebbles thrown at me in the woods and assumed it was people that I couldn't see or hear moving stealthily around. I've come to find out more about Bigfoot lore and have since changed my mind on what or who was throwing pebbles at me. There are a whole lot of ghosts and disturbed spirits as well as ancient ruins in the state, denoting people who have been here for a very long time. But let's not forget the modern age—Utah was settled by the Mormons, a people with a lot of supernatural baggage.

I enjoy asking people about their strange experiences because everyone has a story to tell about *that one time... this weird thing happened here.*

I've heard some great Skinwalker tales from local Navajo and plenty of great Bigfoot stories from people who live outside the city limits. But it goes way beyond that here in Utah.

I'd like to think I was even ahead of the curve on Skinwalker Ranch. In the late '90s I heard Clyde Lewis talking about it on his show, Ground Zero, back when it was broadcast only on Sunday Nights in Salt Lake City on KBER 101. He talked about the Sherman/Gorman Ranch and how people saw portals that had creatures that looked like Bigfoot coming through and roaring. There were giant wolves and UFO-like lights.

I wanted to see that.

So being a rambunctious youth that felt invincible, a friend and I were ready to get prepped and loaded for bear with our gear, guns, and other monster hunting supplies. We talked to Clyde in front of one his favorite haunts–Night Flight Comics– and he said in no uncertain terms, "DO NOT GO!" He explained that the place had been bought by a third party and there would be military-like security guards, and we would be charged with trespassing at the very least.

We didn't go, but I kept that place in the back of my mind, anxiously waiting to hear more about what was going on there.

Twenty-five years on and the place has changed hands to a local Utah realtor magnate. There have been several books, documentaries, and even a miniseries about the ranch, and yet, how much more do we really know? Not much. But the mystery keeps me (and you) coming back, hoping to crack that nut.

David Weatherly has done a phenomenal job tracking down more elusive sources and old tales related to the cryptid creatures that litter the Beehive State. It's inspired me to work on more tales to flesh out some of those bleaching dinosaur bones in the desert. And… I am gonna *have* to track down that Serpent Temple hidden somewhere in the haunted Henry Mountains.

David J. West

Introduction

Utah, the Beehive State. Sitting in the Mountain West region of the U.S., Utah is known for its scenic beauty and rugged mountains. The state slogan—Life Elevated—is, in part, a reflection of the state's vast outdoor spaces.

Utah is a big state—thirteenth largest by area, but it's the 11th least densely populated state in the country. The greatest portion of the state's residents live on the Wasatch Front which includes Salt Lake City. Salt Lake City is also both the state capital and the largest city in Utah.

Ancient Puebloans once lived in the region for thousands of years, and more modern tribes in Utah include the Ute, Goshute, Western Shoshone, Bannock, Navajo, and Southern Paiute.

The area that eventually became Utah was explored by the Spanish in 1540 when they traveled through it during their search for Cibola, the legendary Seven Cities of Gold. In the following years, there were other expeditions into the region, but there was little interest in colonizing it due in part to its rugged desert terrain.

By the early 19th century, European fur trappers were active in the area and in 1825 the city of Ogden was established.

The biggest change for the area came in the summer of 1847 when Brigham Young arrived in the Salt Lake Valley with the first group of Mormon settlers. They had left Illinois after conflicts there and over the next several years, thousands of additional church members arrived in their new home. Even today, Mormons account for just over half of the state's population and it's the only state where a majority of the population belongs to a single church—The Church of Jesus

Christ of Latter-Day Saints—the LDS Church for short.

In the 1840s, settlers in the region learned that California and New Mexico had applied for statehood, so they joined the rush for membership in the Union, attempting to establish the "State of Deseret."

Things didn't go as planned. For a time, the region was officially "Utah Territory." The state of Utah was finally admitted into the Union in 1896, becoming the forty-fifth member of the United States.

The state is landlocked and is bordered by Colorado, Wyoming, Idaho, Arizona, and Nevada. Its bottom southeast corner touches the Northwest corner of New Mexico. The spot has a marker designating the four corners—the spot where four western states meet.

The Beehive State's terrain is varied and ranges from deserts with sand dunes, high mountains, valleys, and forests. Three distinct geological regions converge in Utah: the Great Basin, the Rocky Mountains, and the Colorado Plateau.

The state is known for its spectacular parks including Zion National Park, Bryce Canyon National Park, and Canyonlands National Park. These and other outdoor recreational areas draw tens of thousands of tourists who come to camp, hike, and enjoy other recreations. The state is also home to world renowned ski resorts, the incredible Great Salt Lake, and the Bonneville Salt Flats.

With its vast mountains and wilderness areas, Utah has an abundance of wildlife. The long list of animals to be found in the state includes elk, bighorn sheep, mule deer, coyote, bison, and mountain lions. Smaller mammals range from beaver, fox, and ground squirrels to kangaroo rats and chipmunks.

Bird species range from ravens, jays, and doves to wild turkey and golden eagles. The birder's checklist for Utah is fairly long with many migratory birds visiting the state, as well as numerous other rare birds turning up.

Utah's waters contain plenty of aquatic species including largemouth bass, black crappie, carp, and June sucker.

There are animals that may surprise some people, too—the state reptile is the Gila monster, and the state bird is the California gull.

And then, there are the other creatures that are said to roam the state. With its incredible wilderness areas, it should come as no surprise that Bigfoot has frequently been spotted in Utah. From a famous wave of sightings in South Weber to the high Uinta Mountains, the large, hairy biped is apparently well established in the Beehive.

The state is also home to the famous, or infamous, depending on your view, Skinwalker Ranch. A spot renowned for its UFO activity, the ranch is a hotbed of weird events including numerous unexplainable creature encounters. The ranch itself sits in an area called the Uinta Basin, and it, too, is an area overrun with strange beasts.

Being landlocked, you wouldn't necessarily expect to find a lot of water monster tales in Utah, but there are plenty. From the creepy water babies to strange things in the Great Salt Lake, the Utah Lake monster, and more, the Beehive is rife with unusual aquatic creatures. And let's not forget the Bear Lake Monster—is it real or simply pioneer folklore?

So, join me as we head west and explore the Monsters of the Beehive State.

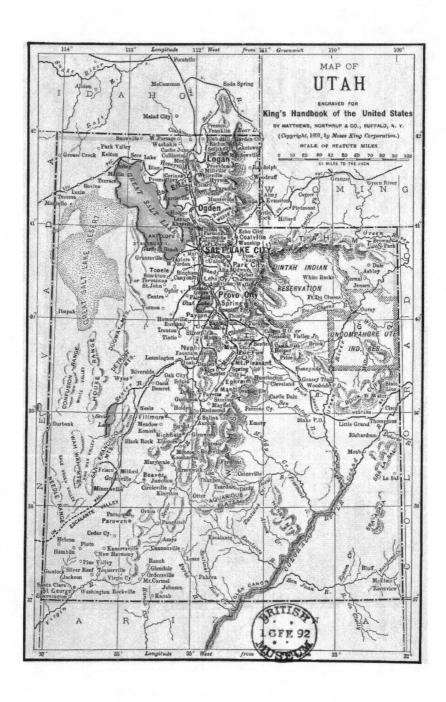

MAP OF

UTAH

ENGRAVED FOR

King's Handbook of the United States

BY MATTHEWS, NORTHRUP & CO., BUFFALO, N. Y.

(Copyright, 1891, by Moses King Corporation.)

SCALE OF STATUTE MILES

0 10 20 30 40 50 60 70 80 90 100

63 MILES TO THE INCH

PART ONE
Hellhounds, Dogmen & Skinwalkers

Wolves and Hellhounds

On September 5, 1919, the *Salt Lake Herald* announced: "Wily Trapper Seeks Scalp of Old Big Foot."

The headline was not a reference to the creature we now commonly associate the name Bigfoot with, i.e. a Sasquatch, rather, it was a story about an elusive wolf that had been preying on sheep in remote areas of San Juan County in the southeastern portion of the state.

A thousand-dollar reward was being offered to the hunter that brought the animal in, a large sum for the day.

The wolf's nickname came from a curious and distinctive flat foot displayed in its tracks, likely the result of either an injury or birth defect.

Wolves were eventually driven out of Utah, but in the pioneer days, they were perceived as a serious threat to both livestock and humans.

In her book, *Folklore in the Bear Lake Valley*, Bonnie Thompson writes about how much early settlers found wolves frightening. Thompson includes comments from Myrtle Rex Jones, a Randolph resident who remembered wolves in Utah from her childhood. She said the creatures were "fiendish, roving and bold," and that they clustered together to hunt. Jones states:

"A cow is helpless in a pack of wolves. They chose only the best to eat, preferably a young yearling heifer freshly killed, and ate only the choice parts. At one time it was estimated that wolves killed 2 percent of the stock in the Valley each year. Many times, the animals seemed to be killed just for amusement."

When she was young, Myrtle and her brother Eldon saw wolves often. She recalls that it was common to see wolf packs roaming across the fields and that the family horse would often stop and wait for the wolves to cross the road and go into the distance before it would move on.

Even the Native Americans in the region claimed the wolves were vicious and dangerous.

The last wolf in Utah was reportedly shot and killed in 1929. There were, over the years, sporadic reports of wolves, but if they were still present in the state, they stayed well hidden.

In 1995 a number of gray wolves were transplanted into Yellowstone National Park and into Central Idaho. Since animals aren't bound by state lines, Utah was eventually affected by the new wolf population in neighboring states. In December 2002 one of the wolves was caught in a trap in Ogden, and in 2004 a pair of wolves was spotted near Vernal.

While these are normal, known creatures, the wolf and canid motif play a big role in some of the strangest cryptid tales to come out of the Beehive State. From real wolves, we turn to stories on the other end of the spectrum—supernatural canids.

A man told me that he was in a cemetery outside of St. George in Washington County in the summer of 1996 when he saw a large black dog prowling around behind the headstones. It was late afternoon, and the man was by himself doing some genealogical research when he spotted the creature. Initially, he brushed it off, thinking the dog belonged to a nearby household, but after a few moments, he started to feel odd. He recounts:

"I didn't give it much thought at first, but the dog kept creeping around behind the headstones. Then I realized that there really weren't many houses close by, so it didn't make sense why the dog was out there unless it was feral. I looked up and saw it staring at me from behind a headstone. It was extremely large, solid black, and its eyes looked red. I got to my car as quick as I could and got out of there. I haven't been back."

What the man described is the classic description of a hellhound—large black dogs often seen around graveyards. Stories of such beasts can be found all over the world. They're believed to be supernatural creatures, interpreted at times as guardians and almost always as representatives of hell, the devil and ill fortune. Bluesman Robert Johnson even sang about them in his 1937 song "Hellhound on my Trail."

Whatever the things are, those who encounter them say they're terrifying and those who encounter them feel lucky to have gotten away without harm.

A report on the *Utah UFO Hunters* website details what sounds like another hellhound incident. This one occurred in Teasdale in Wayne County in 1998.

There were two witnesses in this case, and they, too, were in a cemetery. It was about ten o'clock at night when they spotted a large "dog thing" that seemed fierce and possibly rabid. The creature was reported to be around 4 feet in length, 2-3 feet in height, and weighed approximately 150 pounds.

The witnesses reported hearing growling and snarling coming from the animal and its eyes glowed red. When a flashlight was directed toward the beast, it vanished.

Hellhounds certainly aren't limited to cemeteries; they also seem to enjoy prowling along lonely backroads and highways. A stretch of road in the town of Randlett, south of Fort Duchesne in Uintah County, is known as Dead Man's Curve. Reportedly, the winding road is plagued by a large wolf that appears out of nowhere and runs alongside vehicles. The beast is aggressive and runs at cars as if trying to attack them. Frightened drivers are forced to swerve away and often run off the road trying to avoid the animal. Frequently, it disappears as suddenly as it appeared, leaving puzzled and shaken witnesses questioning their sanity.

Another stretch of highway in Utah known for hellhounds is the infamous Highway 666.

Known variously as the Highway to Hell and the Devil's Highway, the 200 mile stretch of highway crosses three southwestern states, Utah, Colorado, and New Mexico. The highway developed such a stigma over the years that in 2003, the state highway and transportation departments of the three affected states got together and proposed a change in designation for the road. The application was quickly accepted, and U.S. Route 666 became U.S. Route 491.

Despite the change in designation, supernatural legends connected to the highway have persisted, and they are numerous. Some people claim to have lost time while traveling the route. Others speak of ghostly phantoms who appear along the roadway or strange lights that appear and disappear. As should be expected, the demonic theme plays heavily in the highway's legend. A black car that's been dubbed "Satan's Sedan" is said to appear out of nowhere and is known to barrel toward other drivers. If this isn't bad enough, there's also some kind of evil spirit that drives a semi-truck. People say the truck moves at high speed and sometimes its wheels are on fire.

Needless to say, there are also hellhounds that haunt the cursed route. The vicious creatures run in a pack along old 666 and they are aggressive. They leap at vehicles, snap their jaws at tires, and try to force drivers off the road. If someone is foolish enough to drive with an open window, the dogs will try to leap inside the moving vehicle. The animals' eyes are said to glow red or yellow, and their jaws and teeth are reportedly strong enough to puncture the tires of moving vehicles.

Such reports of course border into the supernatural, but many witnesses swear that the animals are physical. One woman told me she clearly heard the sound of one of the animals "thumping against her car" when she was driving the route late one night. According to her, there were five or six of the dogs running together, and they kept pace with her vehicle for what she believed was several miles before they vanished. During that time, she said, the dogs would leap against the vehicle, physically striking it. She believed they were trying to make her run off the highway.

Of course, a lot of people believe that the infamous highway is home to another, even more dreaded creature—the skinwalker.

Utah has many reports of strange wolf-like creatures

Skinwalkers & Dogmen

Skinwalkers are a complicated topic and a full exploration of them would take a hefty text. By no means am I going to attempt here to fully explain the concept of these weird beings. At best, it's a difficult topic to address and understanding them is tricky, especially for non-native people. That being said, legends of skinwalkers are certainly part of the landscape in Utah, so let's consider some basics:

Skinwalkers not limited to Utah by any means, and the most frequent tales of them come from the Navajo Reservation which is primarily in Arizona and New Mexico, with a smaller portion in the state of Utah.

In basic terms, skinwalkers are a type of Navajo witch, but even this statement needs to be clarified. The Diné, commonly known as the Navajo, view witches in the way people of European descent do, and they certainly aren't talking about modern wiccan practitioners.

To the Navajo, witches are evil people. They have fallen out of balance with the world because they are pursuing things of a dark nature, usually related to personal desires, greed, the desire for power, etc.

In Diné, the beings are known as *"yee naaldlooshii,"* and this term, as well as the common "skinwalker," are not words you are likely to hear being spoken by members of the Navajo nation. It's believed that by merely speaking the word, you can attract the attention of these evil beings. And it's not the kind of attention that anyone should want.

To become a skinwalker, an initiate must perform a series of dreadful, even criminal acts. Once completed, the skinwalker gains a wide range of supernatural powers. They are able to imitate human voices, even the voices of those who are deceased. They can also exert a hypnotic, mind controlling influence over their victims.

They are known to utilize "corpse powder" and to fire small bone darts that can cause illness and even death.

As for the name, skinwalker, it's derived from their ability to shapeshift. They do so by donning the skin of another creature. In doing so, their magic allows them to assume the full or partial form of the skin they are wearing. Common forms that the witches utilize include wolf, coyote, dog, and owl. If all of this isn't creepy enough, consider this: a skinwalker can assume the form of another human—if they obtain that person's skin.

Before we get too far down the rabbit hole of supernatural creatures, let's consider this: what people often report as skinwalkers are creatures close to the classic description of the werewolf, and in modern terms, dogman.

Dogman is a term that has come into common use in recent years, and it's sometimes used interchangeably with the term werewolf. Some people dispute this, claiming that while werewolves are shapeshifters, dogmen seem to be an entirely separate species that exists hidden in the wild.

The most well-known "dogman-like" creature is the famous Beast of Bray Road, a creature covered extensively in books by my colleague Linda Godfrey.

Researchers around the country receive accounts from eyewitnesses who say they've had sightings of, and sometimes disturbing encounters with, dogmen.

The creatures are described as bipedal, humanoid canids with a wolf's or dog's snout and pointed ears. Dogmen are said to be aggressive and dangerous.

Some witnesses just aren't sure what to call the creatures that they've encountered. In the state of Utah, tales of dogmen, skinwalkers and even hellhounds converge in a unique way and one of the focal points of these accounts is the Uinta Basin and the infamous Skinwalker Ranch.

Skinwalkers & Dogmen

The old gate leading to Skinwalker Ranch

A Strange Ranch

It would be impossible to write a book about strange creatures in Utah without addressing what is easily the strangest place in the state—the infamous Skinwalker Ranch.

It would take volumes to even begin to address all the purported activity on the ranch and much of it falls into the UFO spectrum. There are, however, numerous accounts of weird creatures on the property, and it's some of these accounts that we'll look at here.

Skinwalker Ranch has long been a hotbed of strange activity. Manifestations range from UFO sightings to poltergeist activity to cattle mutilations and bizarre creature encounters. And that's just the tip of the iceberg!

Skinwalker Ranch is in the Uinta Basin. I've spent time in the region myself, and although most people only talk about the ranch, in part due to the attention it's gained, it's my view that the entire Uintah Basin is a hotbed for high strangeness.

The basin is the most northernly section of the Colorado Plateau and sits at an elevation of 5,000 to 10,000 feet above sea level. Cities in the region include Vernal and Roosevelt as well as numerous other small towns and unincorporated communities. The basin is also the location of the Uintah and Ouray Indian Reservation, home of the Northern Ute tribe.

The Uinta Mountains are on the basin's northern border, and they include the state's highest point, Kings Peak, with a summit of 13,528 feet. The climate in the basin is semi-arid.

Skinwalker Ranch became well known after the publication of *Hunt for the Skinwalker* by Colm A. Kelleher and George Knapp. Subtitled *Science Confronts the Unexplained at a Remote Ranch in Utah*, the book details some of the strange events that took place on the ranch and led millionaire Robert Bigelow to purchase the property.

In the book, the family that Bigelow purchased the property from is named Gorman. This has been a confusing point for some people over the years. The family's real name soon came out—Sherman—but it hasn't prevented some people from being confused by the variation of owner names.

Terry and Gwen Sherman, the people who sold the ranch to Bigelow, experienced disturbing activity on the property and it became so intense that they eventually sold the place just to get away from what they felt was a dangerous situation. Once Bigelow obtained the property, he set up ongoing scientific investigations of the events taking place there.

My friend and colleague Christopher O'Brien was perhaps the first investigator to visit the ranch back when the Shermans still owned the property.

O'Brien is the leading authority on the cattle mutilation phenomenon and has spent decades investigating UFOs and other related topics. O'Brien says of the ranch:

"The Sherman Ranch case is one of the most compelling stories of an ongoing series of paranormal events ever investigated by modern science. It has it all: magic, legends, crypto-creatures, UFOs, aliens, cattle mutilations, portal phenomena, possible abductions, and government intrigue; and the fact that it is centered around what the Utes call 'the path of the skinwalker,' in my mind, makes it even more compelling."

Kelleher and Knapp's book details some of the cryptid related cases that took place on the ranch. One in particular that caught a lot of attention is the tale of a giant, seemingly invulnerable wolf.

A Strange Ranch

The Bulletproof Wolf

There are plenty of bizarre stories from Skinwalker Ranch, but perhaps the best known account is the tale of the bulletproof wolf.

The story takes up the first chapter of *Hunt for the Skinwalker*, and with good reason—it's a creepy and compelling story and it sets the tone for the book's exploration of weird events on the ranch.

The incident took place in 1994 when the Shermans were still in the process of moving everything to their new property.

When the wolf was first spotted, it was seen in the distance but quickly came up to the drive where the Shermans were unloading.

The creature approached the family and acted in a tame, almost docile manner. The family was nervous due to the size of the animal, but it allowed itself to be petted and it was so calm around people that there was immediate speculation that it was perhaps someone's lost pet. Still, something wasn't quite right.

The animal had bright blue eyes and a silver-gray coat that was wet from where it had run through the grass in the field. The wolf was muscular and large, but as the book notes, something was very unusual right off the bat. It was somewhat unsettling that a two-hundred-pound beast was exuding such a calm manner.

As the scene was unfolding, the wolf walked calmly around the family. Nearby was a pen holding a number of prized Angus calves. One of the calves was clearly curious about the wolf and stood watching the scene with its head poking out of the corral bars.

Chaos suddenly erupted. With amazing speed, the wolf shot across to the corral and clamped its jaws on the head of the calf. The family was momentarily paralyzed with shock, but soon sprang into action. The men kicked at the wolf, trying to get it to release the calf, but it was unfazed. Next, a baseball bat was used but solid strikes landed on the creature's back had no effect, and it continued to hold the poor calf in its jaws.

As the wolf pulled at the calf, attempting to yank it through the bars of the corral, the men took the next step needed—they retrieved a firearm. Little did they expect what would happen next.

A powerful .357 Mangum handgun was produced and aimed at the wolf. As *Hunt for the Skinwalker* recounts:

"The shot rang across the field and slammed into the wolf's ribs. The slug from the .357 had no effect whatsoever on the attacking animal. It didn't yelp, didn't pause, and didn't bleed."

Two more shots were fired at close range into the wolf's upper abdomen. Still, the beast held on to the helpless calf.

"On the third shot the wolf slowly and reluctantly released the bleating calf. The calf scampered quickly to the back of the corral and, still bleating, lay down. It was bleeding heavily from the head."

The wolf now stood about ten feet from the men, but it showed no sign of injury despite having been kicked, beaten, and shot numerous times. It stared at the men which they found even more disconcerting. The creature kept looking back at the corral as if considering making another attempt at attacking one of the animals.

A thirty-aught-six was retrieved from the house and again the wolf was shot. The gun could easily bring down large elk and should have easily brought the wolf down, but instead, all the bullet did was cause the creature to step back slightly. The wolf was shot again. This time, a chunk of its flesh splattered off and landed in the grass; but despite this, the animal lived and seemed unaffected. It did, however, finally turn and leave the scene, slowly trotting away across the field.

Sherman and his son decided to pursue the creature. They gave chase and followed as it went toward a stand of cottonwood trees. The beast went through the trees and into a clearing on the other side. All the while, the men kept it in their line of sight as they tried to catch up.

The wolf headed for a cluster of Russian olive trees that bordered a creek. The creature's tracks were clear in the moist soil, and the men made their way through the trees and thorny bushes and emerged near the water. What happened next was even more puzzling. As *Hunt for the Skinwalker* recounts:

"About twenty-five yards from the river, the prints entered a muddy patch, and it appeared as if the two-hundred-pound animal had sunk almost two inches into the mud. The deep paw prints continued for another five yards and then stopped. The tracks simply vanished. So did the wolf. Gone.

There was no explanation for what had happened. A physical creature couldn't just up and vanish in the middle of a muddy patch of land, yet that's exactly what had occurred.

The shaken men returned to the ranch, unable to explain the events. When they examined the chunk of flesh from the wolf, it reportedly looked and smelled line rotten meat. It was yet another puzzle that they tried their best to ignore, hoping to get on with the day-to-day affairs of the homestead.

But they were in for a lot more.

A few weeks after the bulletproof wolf incident, Mrs. Sherman was arriving home from work and had just opened the gate leading up to the homestead. Sitting in her vehicle, she noticed movement in her peripheral vision. She turned and was shocked to see a massive wolf. *Hunt for the Skinwalker* reports her experience:

"As she stared into the friendly light-blue eyes of the huge animal, she felt a knot of fear tighten. The animal's head stood over the roof of her car. This was no ordinary wolf—it resembled the bulletproof animal they had encountered only a few weeks previously."

This time, it wasn't a lone wolf. Farther away from the

A bullet proof wolf is said to roam near Skinwalker Ranch

car was another animal. It wasn't as large as the wolf, but still oversized. Sherman reported that "it looked like a weird dog." The dog's head looked too large for its body.

Sherman hit the gas and raced away from the creatures.

BEEHIVE STATE MONSTERS by David Weatherly

More Tales from the Ranch

Plenty of other strange animals have been spotted around the ranch, including Bigfoot-like creatures, birds that are multicolored and exotic in appearance, and animals that are elusive and difficult to see clearly.

George Knapp's November 21, 2002, article published in the *Las Vegas Mercury*, reported on another weird creature that the Shermans spotted on their ranch, something that was vicious and hyena-like.

The incident occurred one afternoon when the Shermans arrived back at their ranch. Driving onto the property, they spotted something attacking one of their horses. The article says the creature was "'Low to the ground, heavily muscled, weighing perhaps 200 pounds, with curly red hair and a bushy tail.' It somewhat resembled a muscular hyena and seemed to be clawing at their horse, almost playing with it."

Sherman rushed toward the creature, shouting at it as he ran. When he was within forty feet of its location, it vanished.

The Shermans checked on their horse and discovered that the animal had several claw marks on its legs from the attacks it suffered from the weird beast.

According to Knapp: "A few months later, the wife of a deputy sheriff reported seeing a similar muscular, reddish beast running across the property."

During their exploration of events on the ranch, Knapp and Kelleher spoke to a Ute man they call Brandon Ware (not his real name) who had worked as a tribal security officer. The trio discussed both skinwalkers and Sasquatch. While some people in the region are of the opinion that skinwalkers and Sasquatch are the same thing, the security officer was adamant that the two are separate entities. "Skinwalkers are smaller," he said, stating that they were closer to human size while Sasquatch were much larger and overall, less troublesome.

Ware also related a tale that's been frequently repeated involving a pair of cigarette smoking skinwalkers spotted near the ranch. The account is one that some researchers have difficulty accepting simply because it is so bizarre in nature.

A May 9, 2018, article on the *Gaia* website reports the incident:

"Two BIA (Bureau of Indian Affairs) officials were patrolling near the ranch when they saw a pair of 'humanoid' figures standing together on the side of the road. Weirdly, the officers swore the canids were standing upright, wearing trench coats and smoking cigarettes. The patrol pulled over and got out of the car; they looked at each other, but when they looked again, the dogs were gone, leaving smoking cigarette butts on the ground."

It's important to note that this account has been told and retold on numerous websites. In some versions, there is only a single witness who spots the pair of smoking dogmen. Whether or not this implies a second sighting by a witness other than the BIA agents is difficult to say. I have not spoken directly to either of these parties.

Junior Hicks was a legendary Utah researcher who spent years collecting reports of the strange in the Beehive State with a focus on activity in the Uinta Basin.

For years, Hicks was a science teacher at Roosevelt High School. He had a reputation for honesty and integrity and made good connections with locals who quickly learned that he would keep things confidential and take them seriously when they reported their encounters to him. He started collecting reports of anomalous activity in 1951. During his years of research (Hicks passed away in 2020), Hicks became friends with many people in the region, including members of the Ute nation. Hicks stated that some of his Ute friends believed that the skinwalker presence in the Uinta Basin extended back at least fifteen generations.

Conflict between the Utes and the Navajos is said to be rooted far in the past when the Utes reportedly captured Navajos and sold them in slave markets in New Mexico. During the American Civil War, some Ute bands allied themselves with the U.S. military and took part in a campaign against the Navajo led by Kit Carson. These actions led to the Navajo putting a curse on the Utes and sending the dreaded skinwalkers to plague the Ute people.

According to the Utes, the ranch lies "on the path of the skinwalker," and because of this, the property is off-limits to tribal members.

In his book *Stalking the Tricksters*, Christopher O'Brien notes that Junior Hicks tried on many occasions to gain access to a place called Dark Canyon. The canyon is on Ute land not far from the ranch and, according to some tribal members, it's where the skinwalker lives. The area is considered taboo and Hicks was denied access. A tribal elder later told Hicks that the tribe didn't want anything to disturb the skinwalker because it could cause serious problems.

Purportedly, there are ancient petroglyphs in the canyon, some of which depict skinwalkers. Hicks isn't the only person who has tried to gain access to the location over the years, but the tribe has turned down every request.

More Strange Canids

Hicks told me about a dogman encounter reported to him by two young women near the town of Roosevelt, though he didn't specify the date of the sighting.

The women were at a graveyard near the town when they saw a wolf-like creature standing on two legs staring at them. The women were frightened by the beast and ran to the safety of their vehicle. Speeding away from the area, they were even more shocked to see that the creature was pursuing them. Running on two legs, the thing was close to the car and keeping pace, despite the speed that they were traveling.

The terrified women continued at a high rate of speed, and the dogman kept pace with the vehicle for several miles. Finally, the creature veered off in another direction and vanished into the darkness.

The women described a werewolf-like creature with dark fur and pointed ears like a wolf or dog.

Another story I've heard from several sources sounds right out of a classic werewolf movie. Reportedly, another dogman was spotted in the town of Roosevelt where it was leaping from rooftop to rooftop. Numerous people are said to have witnessed this event, and in some versions of the account, authorities gave chase to the creature but were unable to capture it.

As intriguing as the account is, I've been unable to locate any of the witnesses who were on hand for the event. This being the case, there are no further details available.

A Colorado man wrote to my colleague Linda Godfrey about a skinwalker tale from his family. The account is detailed in Godfrey's book *I Know What I Saw*.

The man's heritage is Ottawa and Ute, and his mother grew

up in eastern Utah. The correspondent noted that he had spent many childhood summers in a small town near Skinwalker Ranch. He told Godfrey about an incident reported by his aunt:

"My aunt used to tell me about an encounter she had with what she believed was a skinwalker up near an area north of Roosevelt in the Uinta Mountains called Moon Lake. An upright canine creature with red eyes kept pace with her car along a gravel road. She lost it [the creature] when she hit the paved road and sped off."

The man also told Godfrey that locals in the area had long reported that Moon Lake was another hot spot for skinwalker activity.

Lon Strickler's book *Phantoms and Monsters: Mysterious Encounters* contains an account from Mike, a man who said his grandfather had an encounter with a skinwalker. Mike reports that his grandfather lived in Myton, a small town in Duchesne County, and that when he visited him, the old man would sometimes tell stories about skinwalkers.

Mike asked his grandfather if he had ever encountered a skinwalker, and the old man replied that he had. When he was "young and foolish," the man went to a location known as "Skinwalker Valley," a spot that others stayed well away from. He told his grandson that the place was very strange with black trees that looked dead but were still living, and grass that looked like it had been burned.

In this weird place, the man discovered a house with no door and a caved-in roof. Mike recounts:

"There were marks on the sides of the house. Animal skeletons were everywhere around the house as if it were a sacred burial ground. He then heard her. His grandmother. She had died long ago, but he heard her."

The man became frightened and fled the area but according to Mike, his grandfather never really got away. The skinwalkers didn't forget the man and his trespass. Mike relates:

"Whenever I visited him, he would have something of his that was brand new broken the next day, crushed or killed. He finally stopped keeping his dogs outside."

Mike reports that his grandfather once showed the boy his back, covered with what appeared to be marks from some kind of claws. This upset the young boy and when Mike's mother took him and left, he saw something that has remained burned in his memory:

"I saw a black dog with white eyes. It was watching him [the grandfather] and he was watching it as if waiting for it to come to him. It never did.

"I never saw that dog again. My grandpa died two months later. They said his heart gave out, but I knew that was a lie. His arm had fresh marks and his dog died from loneliness, it was still a pup."

A posting on the *Skinwalker Ranch* Online Forum details a weird encounter that took place in either 1992 or 1993.

The reporting witness was one of four college students on a spring break trip in southern Utah. They were driving at night on I70 traveling from Saint George to Moab. Conditions were clear but the pleasant drive was interrupted when the vehicle overheated. The group was stuck on the side of the road while they waited for the engine to cool.

The driver got out of the car to relieve himself. Moments later, he came running back to the vehicle, screaming in panic that "something" was out there. He jumped back in the driver's seat and started turning the engine over trying to start the car. The reporting witness was in the back seat. He recalls what he saw:

"I saw a huge black shape behind the fence. He [the driver] got in the car and began to try and start the car. I watched as this 7-8-foot-tall creature covered in hair just walked over or maybe it leaped over the fence. It approached the car and stood maybe 15 feet away. We were all screaming at this time for him [the driver] to get moving.

"I noticed its eyes were red and seemed like hot coals floating in this black hairy silhouette. It had either long ears that poked up above the top of its head or it had horns."

The driver got the car started and sped away from the creature. The witness says that he continued to look at the creature as they drove away from it. It stood on the side of the road watching the vehicle. The witness said the creature's glowing eyes were visible for some distance.

A sighting reported on the *Utah UFO Hunters* website comes from a witness who spotted a pair of large hyena-like dogs in the summer of 2003. The creatures were seen feeding on a dead deer along Highway 40 near Roosevelt in Duchesne County. It was around ten o'clock in the morning on June 21.

The witness stopped the vehicle to get a better look at the creatures and they ran from the scene. He had his daughter with him, and she thought that one of the animals was injured since she saw blood on it.

The creatures were dog-like, though the man stated, "I have never seen dogs like this." He noted that both the shape and size of the creatures was unusual. Additionally, he reported that the animals had "weird coloring" that was black and gray. He estimated that they weighed between 75 and 90 pounds. The creatures had no tails.

"What made them different from dogs was body shape and the way they held themselves and they ran almost like rabbits. It stuck with me since we saw them, and I keep asking people if there could be hyenas in this area and they get a good laugh out of it."

Another report on the *Utah UFO Hunters* site involves a creature described as having black, long, frizzy hair, yellow reflective eyes and pointed ears. The creature had no tail and was able to move both bipedally and on all fours in an ape-like fashion.

Three witnesses spotted the creature on July 26, 2003, along Highway 89. They were traveling from Hyrum to Logan at the time and it was around ten o'clock at night.

The creature moved extremely quickly, and the witnesses reported hearing a "screeching" sound coming from the animal.

A man named Grant Tuft wrote to Linda Godfrey in 2012

after hearing her discuss werewolves and dogmen on a radio show. Tuft told Godfrey that he'd had an encounter with an upright canine in Utah in 2003.

Tuft was coaching football at Enterprise High School, forty-five miles from his home in Cedar City. As a result, he always had a bit of a drive after late night games.

On a Friday night in mid-October, the man left the school around one a.m. for his trek home. His drive was on a rural country road and there were no businesses, houses, or streetlights.

There was often a lot of wildlife in the area, so the man was driving cautiously and watching carefully lest a deer run out in the road. He was about halfway through his drive when something ahead caught his attention. As detailed in *I Know What I Saw*:

"I could see something walking just off the shoulder of the road. I slowed in case whatever it was ran across the open road. At first, I thought it was a big dog, but as I got closer, I knew there was no way it could be. It was huge. I don't really know what to compare it to in size. I guess a bear would be a good comparison. If it stood upright, it would have been easily over six feet tall. I know it wasn't a bear because it didn't look like a bear or walk like a bear. It walked like a dog."

As the man got closer to the figure, he started wondering why a dog was out in the middle of nowhere. He started to slow down more, wanting to get a better look at the animal. As he approached, he saw that its fur was thick and black or brown in color. He told Godfrey the fur was "kind of shaggy." He could tell that the animal's head was canid in shape, though it was very large.

"As I was almost up to it, it turned and looked in my direction and that scared me. My skin crawled and my hair stood up. Its eyes were red! Like a stoplight. As I passed, I was looking at it and it looked directly in my eyes. At that point I hit the gas and sped away from it as fast as I could."

Tuft told Godfrey that the incident has remained ingrained in his memory and that the creature's eyes still give him goose

"It stood upright…it walked like a dog."

bumps.

In 2007, I interviewed a Duchesne County man about a disturbing encounter that took place on his farm.

On a Friday morning in mid-October 2003, the man's twenty-year-old son went out to tend to the family's animals. It was just after sunrise and the man was surprised to find the sheep huddled around the fence as close to the house as they could get. The animals were acting very strange, and it was clear that something was wrong, so the young man called his father to help assess the situation.

The older man quickly did a count of the flock and determined that one animal was missing. The two men herded the animals into a barn and set out to search the fields for the missing sheep.

The old farmer's first thought was that something— possibly a mountain lion—had made off with the missing animal and that the attack had frightened the rest of the sheep. The man expected to find tracks and possibly other signs from the attack. What he didn't expect was what he and his son discovered in the pasture.

The body of the missing sheep was on the ground. It had been viciously attacked. Something had torn the animal open and eaten many of the internal organs. Searching the area, the men found prints around the dead animal, but they weren't the expected mountain lion tracks. A careful examination of the prints left the farmer believing that his sheep had been attacked and killed by a very large canine.

Realizing that he was dealing with either a wolf or a feral dog, the man decided to keep his sheep in the barn and wait to see if the predator returned for another meal that night.

In shifts, the men took turns through the night, planted firmly out of sight near the house with a good view of the pasture where their animal had been killed. Rifles in hand, they waited.

All was quiet until early morning when the sun was rising. The man's son was on watch and saw something moving over the rise at the back of the field. He nudged his father awake and they watched as the animal slowly made its way toward them. It was clearly a canid of some kind, and it was the largest the farmer had ever seen.

The closer it got, the more unnerved the man became. Finally, when it was in easy shooting range, the man zeroed in on it with the scope of his gun. The animal stopped as if it sensed the men.

The farmer eyed the creature through the scope of his gun. As he was doing so, the thing rose up on its hind legs and looked straight at the man. Too shocked to fire, the farmer could only watch, slack jawed, as the animal bounded away on two legs, quickly darting into the trees and out of sight.

When I interviewed the two men, I found them both credible. Recounting their experience years after the event, they were still clearly shaken by the memory of the strange creature.

An article on the website *Hunt the Skinwalker* reports that late in October 2008 a man named Lamar Oaks and his son Craig were out on their property doing some target practice when they spotted what they first thought was a wild dog or coyote. Concerned about the safety of their farm animals, the men fired at the creature. Both were certain that they hit it. As reported on the website:

"Then things became bizarre. Instead of the animal falling over, it stood up on its hind legs and looked deliberately at the astonished pair. The movement, according to Lamar, was 'intentional and graceful.'"

During interviews with the witnesses, the two men both said the creature was thin and wolf- or coyote-like in appearance with a thick, bushy tail. Its hair was long, coarse, and reddish in color. It had dog-like paws and the hind legs were angled and curved. Lamar said the creature's front legs were retracted toward its chest "like a kangaroo."

Regaining their composure, the men raised their guns to fire at the creature again. It fled the area, running away on two legs and heading toward a creek.

The Oaks' pit bull pursued the creature but was unable to keep pace with it. The men saw the dogman cross the creek and vanish into a stand of Russian Olive trees.

According to the online report, Skinwalker Ranch investigators interviewed numerous people in the area over a three-year period (2008-2011) and discovered that many other witnesses had seen similar creatures in the region.

In late 2009 I was contacted about a purported haunted residence in Vernal, Uintah County. The man living at the property told me that his family was experiencing poltergeist-like activity that included disembodied voices, objects in the home moving, and other strange phenomena.

The man told me that he had seen an "unusual wolf" lurking around the back of the property. The man was an experienced outdoorsman and he insisted that it was not a normal, known animal of any kind. Oddly, each time the animal appeared, paranormal activity in the home increased for the following two days.

The creature was spotted both on all fours and standing upright on its hind legs. The man told me that the creature unnerved him, and he always had a bad feeling when it showed up. He recalled one incident from a Friday morning in the fall—sometime between four and five a.m. his dog started barking wildly and tearing around the house. The man went downstairs, gun in hand, because he thought someone might be trying to break into the home. He watched as his dog ran from one room to another, behaving in an alarmed manner.

Finding no signs of intrusion, or anything else amiss in the house, the man stepped out into the back yard. Scanning the area, he spotted what he thought was a wolf at the edge of the property. As he watched, the wolf rose up on its hind legs, standing completely upright next to a large tree. He told me:

"I had the gun in my hands, but I didn't even think about shooting that thing. I was so stunned by what I was seeing. I hunted for years. I've seen bear, mountain lion, coyotes, wolves, all kinds of things in the wild. That was not a normal creature."

The man's dog, who had been at his side, turned and

retreated back inside the house.

The creature stood upright for a few moments, then went back down to all fours and took off, quickly vanishing from his line of sight. The man said that he was shaken up for a couple of days after seeing the creature.

Given that the wolf was next to a tree, the man was able to get a good estimate of the thing's height. He showed me where it had stood and reported that it was about seven feet tall. There was a mark on the tree that was believed to have been left by the wolf.

The creature was seen on about a half dozen occasions, usually at the back half of the property.

During one of my visits to the home, I posted a trail camera at the back of the property, hoping to get a photo of the creature.

Not long after, the man contacted me and said that he and his family had heard strange growling noises in the backyard the previous night, from the area where the bipedal wolf had been spotted and where the camera was posted.

Despite that fact that the camera was well secured on a tree, it disappeared. The camera was later located about a half a mile from its original location, strapped to a tree in the middle of nowhere.

Oddly, there were no tracks or signs around either the camera's original location or the spot where it had been relocated. There were no signs of animal or human presence.

As for photos, the camera was empty, not a single shot had been snapped even though test shots showed that it remained in perfect working condition.

Another reported incident was even more disturbing for the family involved. The man told me he believed the creature was on the roof of the home one night and the sounds of the thing walking on the roof could be heard clearly.

Concerned for the safety of his children, the man soon moved his family out of the house. The family who took over the residence would not discuss whether or not activity continued on the property once they took up residence.

Another article on *Hunt the Skinwalker* details an encounter from June 4, 2011. According to the account, Riana Smith, Blake Bagley, and their infant son were traveling north on 6500 East north of Fort Duchesne around 9:30 in the evening when a panicked cow ran out in front of their vehicle.

Black was driving the car and quickly slammed the brakes but was unable to stop before hitting the animal. The cause of the cow's panic appeared to be another creature that was illuminated by the car's headlights: "a large wolf-like creature approximately six feet tall that ran on two legs into the road next to the prostate cow and continued running across the road in front of both astonished witnesses."

The two witnesses were interviewed separately, and both described a tall canid with a head and shoulders that resembled a German shepherd or wolf. The creature had dark brown or black hair that was long. It moved quickly and easily on two legs and passed within a couple of feet of the cow that had been struck.

When first spotted, the creature was pursuing the cow. Once it was caught in the car's headlights, it changed direction and rapidly vanished into the darkness.

According to the online report, the accident was filed with authorities and verified. Investigators went to the scene to look for evidence of the creature. The report notes:

"No evidence or unusual footprints were found at the scene. This case, if taken on its own, would inspire skepticism in most people. However, beginning in 2008, dozens of cases involving dogmen walking on two legs were relayed to SR (Skinwalker Ranch) investigators.

So, what exactly are we to make of all these strange canid creatures? Are they dogmen, skinwalkers, werewolves or something else entirely? In speaking with witnesses, it's interesting to note a few things: most people aren't familiar with the term dogman and hesitate to use the term "werewolf" since it harkens to movie monsters. The term skinwalker carries a whole different set of connotations. The average person isn't usually familiar with it either, and those who are often hesitate to use the word because of various superstitions associated with it. This being the case, witnesses often do their best to describe the creatures without knowing what to call the things they have seen.

Perhaps the creatures like it that way.

The strange activity in the region has puzzled researchers and scientists for years. Maybe, with continued time and patience we will gain more insight and understanding, but until then, we are left with bizarre and sometimes unsettling tales.

PART TWO
Bigfoot in the Beehive

Early Accounts

With its vast amount of wilderness and richness of natural resources, Utah is a perfect place for the elusive Bigfoot.

Reports of Bigfoot in Utah during the early 1900s and up to 1950s are very scant. There are grains of accounts here and there, many of them simply too bare bones to report here. Of course, sighting reports have increased in recent years due to the amount of interest in the cryptid.

The earliest recorded tale involves some lumber men working at a timber camp in Ephraim Canyon. The group encountered an aggressive creature that harassed their camp over several nights. Activity started one night when the men heard strange sounds in the woods around their camp. It was clear that something was moving around, and whatever it was, it was as big as a bear. The camp's dogs barked in alarm at the noises and as the movement continued, the men started catching glimpses of the creature just at the edge of the camp's fire. The men stoked the fire to make it larger in an effort to keep the beast at bay. The following day, the men investigated and discovered the creature's large tracks around the camp.

One night some of the dogs pursued the beast into the woods. They were killed one by one. Afterwards, the camp horses started making noises and soon, they too fell silent.

The frightened men built a large bonfire and fired their guns into the woods around them, hoping to scare the monster away.

The following morning, the bodies of the dogs were discovered; some of them had been tossed forty feet up into the trees. The horses were also dead.

The account seems to be folkloric, but there are at least

some grains of truth to the tale. The timber camp was real and was connected to the construction of the Manti Temple for the LDS church. This would place the account around 1876-77.

It's unclear where the account originated, though the *Utah Bigfoot Blog* lists the source of the tale as an interview with Alan Stock by Kenneth Holm, Merrill-Cazier Library, Special Collections, Folklore Collection #84, Utah State University.

Another early account comes from the 1880s and centers around Gorilla Ridge and Gorilla Creek in the Tushar Mountains northeast of Beaver in Beaver County. Both names are said to come from an old unshaven miner who used to live in the area.

Reportedly, the miner was so unkempt that he resembled a gorilla, hence the name for the two geographic features. But some lore claims the names didn't come about because of the miner. Some tales indicate that some miners in the 1880s spotted a strange creature in the area. They called the creature a gorilla since it was the closest thing in the animal world that fit what they witnessed. It's notable that there was also a mine in the region known as the "Gorilla Mine," presumably named after the same figure or creature.

The *Sasq-Wasatch* website lists a sighting from the late 1930s that occurred in Ogden Valley at the head of Shanghai Canyon. A crew working on the Pineview Dam spotted a small, hairy creature sitting on the rock cliffs above their site. The men spotted the creature several days in a row and even nicknamed him "Pedro." The account was collected by researcher Dave Carver who spoke with one of the dam workers. Although the man was in his eighties when Carver spoke with him, he had never forgotten the strange little creature.

Bigfoot researcher Ron Johnson interviewed Joey, a businessman from Price who recounted a Bigfoot sighting from the 1950s. According to the account, in 1955, the witness's family was taking a trip to Salt Lake City. They left before dark and were traveling up Price Canyon. At the time, the road was still narrow and known as a dangerous route, so drivers took extra care while navigating it.

Just before they reached Ford Creek Falls, the family saw

what they thought was a man standing on the left side of the road. The driver, Joe, stopped the vehicle and he and his son got out to see if it was someone who needed help.

Before they reached the figure, Joey's father suddenly turned and shouted at his son to get back in the car. As Johnson's report on his *Utah Bigfoot Files* website details:

"The man they thought was on the side of the road wasn't a man at all, but some kind of a big beast...the beast never threatened them, moved, nor made a noise of any kind while all of this was taking place."

Joe and his son quickly got back in the vehicle and drove away.

Pressed for details, Joey described the creature to Johnson:

"It stood approximately nine feet tall, much bigger than an average man, very muscular and looked something like a giant ape or gorilla."

There have long been rumors about Bigfoot activity on the Uintah and Ouray Indian Reservation near Roosevelt. One particular canyon is said to be a hotspot for Bigfoot activity, but the land is considered sacred and is strictly monitored by tribal authorities. To date, no outside investigators have been allowed to search for the creatures on native land.

Ute legends also mention the creatures living in the Island Lake area in the High Uintas. The creatures are said to be somewhat aggressive and are known to throw rocks at anyone intruding on their territory.

Bigfoot researcher Ray Crowe reported that an unusual skull had been found in a dry creek bed at the edge of Saint George, Washington County, in southern Utah. The location was near Zion National Park and purportedly the skull was thousands of years old.

The skull was said to have huge brow ridges and a sloping forehead. Speculation was that it was an undiscovered Neanderthal.

In its July 21, 2007, edition, *The Salt Lake Tribune* ran a story about a BFRO (Bigfoot Field Researchers Organization) expedition in the Beehive State. The searchers were following up on a number of reported Bigfoot sightings along Mirror Lake Highway the same week. The paper notes that the area had a long history of sightings:

"When Oakley resident Melissa Morrison used to come to Summit County as a child for family reunions, her uncle told her campfire stories about seeing Sasquatch wandering through the Uinta Mountains."

Bigfoot Through the Decades

1960s

A man wrote to the BFRO to report an encounter he'd had as a child in the Beehive State. The incident took place in the Wasatch Mountains in 1962. The man's father was stationed at Hill Air Force Base at the time. The family, along with some guests, were on a trip to a ski area one spring weekend and stopped to have an early picnic. The witness recalls that it was around nine or ten in the morning and the group stopped in the Wasatch National Forest.

The boy, along with three other children around his age, started playing hide and seek in an open field. After about twenty minutes of play, things took a strange turn for the boy. As he explains:

"There was a small mound on the west side of where we were playing, and I thought that would be a great spot to hide. As the counting began, I ran around the mound and was trying to hide when I got the feeling I was being watched.

"I turned around and about thirty feet from me, standing beside a large tree and bush, was a very large creature. It was just standing there watching me and I was looking at it. It didn't make any aggressive moves or sounds...it was just content watching me. It had reddish-brown long hair all over its body. Dark eyes, and [it was] fairly tall."

The boy started walking backwards to get away from the creature. He and the beast locked eyes and he recalls feeling like he was in a sort of trance. After a moment, he suddenly felt that the situation was dangerous. He reports:

"Some feeling inside of me told me this was not a safe situation and that's when I broke off the stare and ran as fast as

I could. I ran right past my friends and started screaming all the way down the mountain."

The boy told his father that he had seen some kind of creature but wasn't sure what it was. The father went and investigated, but by that time, the creature had vanished.

Curiously, the boy spotted the beast again later that day. He recalls the incident:

"Later on, as we were leaving the area, I happened to look up at that part of the mountain we were playing on and there it was again in the same spot...watching us leave! Before I could say anything, we rounded the corner and lost sight of it."

The witness says that, due to the incident, he was afraid to go into the woods alone for many years. It was much later in his life that he saw a picture of Bigfoot and recognized that it was the creature that he had spotted that spring day.

The *Utah UFO Hunters* website has a report from a witness who had a sighting in Farmington Canyon in Davis County in 1966.

The large black creature was seen moving at an estimated speed of 40 mph and easily leaping over three-foot-high sage brush. The creature was in view for less than ten seconds and it quickly hid behind some trees at the base of a hill.

The reporting witness, and two companions, were about 500 yards from the creature and a strong, foul stench was in the air, presumably coming from the beast.

A report on the *Utah Bigfoot* website comes from Doug Wilson who says he and his companions saw an unusual creature on Powder Mountain Road in 1967.

Wilson and two others were in a pickup truck hunting deer. They were aiming a spotlight up the mountain and their attention was drawn to a pair of glowing eyes about 125 yards up the hill from their position on the road. Wilson recalls:

"We stopped the truck and had the spotlight up there. It looked like a person sitting on the side of the hill with their arms over their knees just staring down at us. There was no light-colored clothing or anything, it was all dark. We could just see those eyes looking at us.

The Wasatch Mountains

"We just kind of got out of there. We still never talk about that very much to this day. It's just a little experience that you see something that you don't know what to think about it. A little bit out of the ordinary."

A woman had an encounter with a prowling Bigfoot in Wheeler Canyon, Weber County, in 1968.

On a fall night, the woman was home with her two-year-old son who was asleep at the time. It was late evening, and the woman had been watching television. She walked into the kitchen for a drink and when she went back to her living room, she was startled to see a pair of red, glowing eyes staring at her through a window. Whatever it was, it was peering through the window directly behind the chair she had been sitting in while watching television. A porch light was also on which gave her a partial view of the creature. She told the BFRO:

"All I could see of it was mainly a very dark mass outlined in the window and the eyes which were reflecting the light and seemed to glow red. I stood in the kitchen doorway frozen. I kept trying to tell myself I was seeing things and it wasn't really there."

The woman turned back into the kitchen and took a few moments to calm down, thinking that if it was her imagination, the figure would be gone after she calmed herself; however, when she turned back to the living room again, the lurking creature was still at the window.

The shaken woman walked back to the bedroom where her son was asleep and telephoned for help, telling authorities only that there was a prowler around her house. It took 30-45 minutes before officers with the sheriff's department showed up to investigate.

While she was waiting for the officers, the woman heard several windows on the east side of the house rattle, then the back door shook as if someone, or something, was trying to find a way into the house.

On the surface, the case seems like it could be explained by there being a human prowler around the woman's home, but there are some interesting, additional facts. The report notes:

"They (the deputies) asked for a description, and I said I couldn't see the person because they were standing on the top step next to the porch light and all I could see was a dark outline of their head and shoulders in the window. One of the deputies was about my husband's height, 6'3", and he stood on the top step and the window framed only his head. They commented that my prowler must be fairly tall."

The woman told her husband about the incident, but he initially laughed it off.

"My husband later told me that about a month or so after

that he had a strange encounter early one morning. He was up getting ready for work when he heard a racket out on the porch, so he went out to chase our cats out and stop the noise. As he walked toward the front door, he saw a dark, hairy face looking in at him through the little diamond shaped window in the door."

Thinking it was a bear, the man rushed to the bedroom and retrieved his firearm. When he went back to the door, the creature was gone. The man started thinking about the incident and realized that a bear's snout would not allow it to put its face so close to the window like the creature he had seen did.

The incident left him both puzzled and unsettled and caused him to think again about the experience his wife had reported.

1970s

Utah Bigfoot researcher Ron Johnson spoke with a man who saw a Bigfoot in Price Canyon, Carbon County, in the early 1970s.

Paul Pugliese, a business owner in Price, told Johnson that he and his cousin were riding dirt bikes down Lower Fish Creek when the incident occurred. The pair were near Scofield Reservoir and were making their way down the canyon when Paul got a bit ahead. He stopped to wait for his cousin and when he turned and looked back, he saw a large creature pacing his cousin's dirt bike.

The creature was about eight feet tall and looked like a gorilla. By the time the other rider reached Paul's position, the creature had crossed the river and was climbing the side of the canyon heading northwest.

Paul pointed the thing out to his cousin and both boys took off out of the canyon as quickly as they could.

In 1973, a Weber County man named Craig R. Johnson was out in the Manti-La Sal Mountains elk hunting with some friends. One night something visited their camp, lifted the door off a 300-pound horse trailer, and pitched it ten feet away. There was a vague imprint on the door, but the hunters couldn't determine what the impression was from. A local bear hunter examined the impression and said it was like nothing he had ever seen before.

Johnson also reported that while the hunting party was away from camp the following day, something picked up a full can of beer off a wheel well, bit the can, and replaced it where it was. "The thing that was funny was the fact the beer can showed teeth marks, but was not punctured, just split," Johnson said. (*Ogden Standard-Examiner* February 27, 1980).

A man camping at Millers Flat in Emery County in 1974 told researcher Ron Johnson about a memorable encounter with a Bigfoot.

The witness, Jim, went out at the end of the camping season, expecting to have the area mostly to himself. He set up his camp for the weekend, and in short order, his dog started acting strange and hid under the trailer, refusing to come out.

Jim decided to go for a walk, but about 100 feet from his site, he discovered large, human-like tracks. Although he didn't have anything to measure the prints with, he estimated they were around sixteen inches in length.

Jim grew nervous looking at the tracks and he became even more disturbed when he suddenly felt like he was being watched. He looked around and saw something moving in the trees about fifty feet ahead of his position. He told Johnson that the creature looked "something like a big ape or gorilla."

Jim quickly returned to his trailer, packed his things, and left the area.

Two men hunting in Box Elder County on September 15, 1976, had a disturbing encounter involving a large, hairy aggressive creature.

The reporting witness told the BFRO that the first indication of something strange was a loud "thunk, thunk, thunk" sound that resembled a large boulder hitting the ground.

The man said his companion was stuck in a cluster of thorns and did not see the creature on the hillside above him. He reports:

"It was about 400 yards above Kenny and running toward him. I'll admit my heart was in my throat. I started yelling at Kenny to get out of there and kept repeating it at the top of my lungs. Kenny finally heard me and the noise coming toward him and ran through those thorns...he was halfway through the thorns and must have accidentally fired the shotgun. At that point, I saw it [the creature] stop and start running the other way."

Although Kenny didn't see the creature himself, he was shaken by the incident and refused to talk about it for almost two weeks afterwards. The reporting witness described the creature that he saw:

"I would say it was 7-8 feet tall, dark reddish-brown hair with a white cap. The distance was about 500-600 yards away and closer as it came toward Kenny."

A pair of men hiking the Timpanogos Mountain Range in Wasatch County had some strange experiences in the summer of 1977.

It was sometime in June when the pair headed up to hike the area. They arrived at night, planning to sleep in their car so they could get an early start the following morning.

While they were sitting in the vehicle talking, they heard someone walking behind the car. The driver called out and asked who was there, but there was no response. Moments later, someone, or something, pushed the back of the car down.

Thinking that someone was playing a prank, the driver started the car and turned it around so that the headlights were shining on the area in question. The men observed the shadow of a figure moving through the nearby meadow.

The men searched the area but found no other people or vehicles around. They were disturbed by the incident and returned home that night.

They arrived back at the site early the next morning and proceeded with their planned hike.

About a mile and a half up the trail, they discovered prints in the snow that went off the trail and straight up the side of the hill. The witness reported his encounter on the *Bigfoot Encounters* website. The man reported that he is 6' 1" and was unable to match the stride of the footprints they discovered that day.

The pair reached a point at the base of some cliffs and got the distinct impression that they were being watched. The snow became too deep for the men to continue, and they were concerned about avalanche risk, so they returned to their vehicle.

A mile back down the trail, they noticed a horrible smell that the witness said was like the stench from a rotting animal. Along with the odor came the feeling of being watched again, prompting the hikers to pick up their pace and leave the area.

The September 2, 1977, edition of the *Davis County Clipper* details an encounter from July 10 of that year involving two couples who reportedly spotted a trio of Bigfoot creatures playing around Elizabeth Lake in Davis County.

Mr. and Mrs. Robert Melka, from Bountiful, and Sgt. and Mrs. Fred Rosenberg, from Hill Air Force Base, reported that they were sitting on a ridge half a mile southwest of Elizabeth Lake. The witnesses told reporters:

"We sat on a ridge looking into a meadow 300 to 500 yards away when he saw the first creature. A few seconds later, a second beast—both much larger than humans—entered the meadow. The two romped back and forth in the clearing for at least 10 minutes."

The creatures were bipedal and human-like with arms, legs, and bodies much like a person, but covered with hair. Only the hands and feet were free of hair.

One creature stood in a cluster of pine trees about 100 yards away at the edge of the meadow while the other two played in the open area. They reportedly ran with "tremendous strides." The creatures were between eight and ten feet tall and had rounded heads and broad shoulders. The witness was positive the creatures were not known animals.

"They could not have been bears or other animals. They

did not have pointed snouts as bears do, and we had a good, long look at their profiles. At first, we were shocked by the huge size of these things, but then we became intrigued and just stood and watched them."

About seventeen miles from the location of the Melka/ Rosenberg sighting, one of the Beehive state's most notable Bigfoot encounters occurred on August 22, 1977.

8 Hikers Spot Elusive 'Big Foot' In High Uintahs

AUG 2 5 1977

By BERT STRAND
Outdoor Editor

Two North Ogden men and six young companions said today they watched a "gorilla-like" creature in the High Uintah Mountains that matched reports of "Big Foot."

Jay Barker of 1350 E. 2600 N., who has hunted big game animals for years in the area, said the creature was estimated at being 10 feet tall.

He said it was covered with a white mantle of hair over its

like" imprints in the earth, b the ground was too hard an dry to leave a clear imprint.

He said the paw mark wa "huge" and resembled tha made by a palm and toes. Th party followed the path of th creature to the timber an found other scruff marks rocks and in the dry ground ar grass.

HEAVY TIMBER

Mr. Barker said the grou thought better about followir the hairy creature into t

Eight hikers, including North Ogden residents Jay Barker and Larry Beeson along with six youngsters, were in the Cuberant Basin of the Uinta Mountains when they spotted an eight- to ten-foot-tall creature with white hair. The beast was 600 to 800 yards away from their position and they observed it for about twenty minutes.

While they were watching the strange figure, one of the party accidentally kicked a rock loose and the resulting noise attracted the creature's attention. Alerted that it was being observed, the creature left the area.

Barker and the group investigated the area and discovered a partially eaten rabbit near where they had seen the creature.

Conservation officer Don Paul was informed about the sighting and was at least impressed by the credibility of the witnesses, noting that they were individuals who spent a lot of time in the outdoors.

Terry Parkin and Jerry Dahlberg, officers with the Utah Division of Wildlife Resources, launched a search for the beast, stating that they intended to search for tracks or any other physical signs of the creature—whatever it was.

A few days later, an expedition was launched to search the region, but nothing was found. The area where the thing had been sighted was hard ground, so no tracks were discovered.

The sighting led to a flurry of news articles, and monster hunters converged on the area and scoured the mountains looking for evidence of the creature.

It's important to mention that the Melka/Rosenberg group had kept their encounter quiet, not wanting to face ridicule because of what they had seen. Once the Barker party's encounter hit the news, the two couples decided to come forward and share their report.

A reporter with Ogden's *Standard-Examiner* spoke with the couples separately and found that their stories matched.

The account from the Barker party gained widespread attention and the September 3, 1977, edition of the *Ogden Standard-Examiner* reported that a party of Bigfoot experts was coming to the mountains to conduct a search for the creature.

The paper's outdoor editor, Bert Strand, reported that Cuberant Basin at the head of the Weber River would be the focal point of the search. The article mentioned the sighting by Jay Barker's group and reported:

"Since the report by the group, others have said they spotted a similar creature in other areas of the Uintah Mountains.

"Others in the Cuberant Basin area, two weeks ago, said they heard 'strange' growling and howling in the area. They said the sounds were like nothing they had heard before and they were frightening. They also heard heavy crashing in the brush and timber at the same time."

The paper also reported that Jay Barker had returned to the basin a week prior to the article and noticed a "strange smell" throughout the area.

Strand said that wildlife officials were speculating that the creature was a grizzly bear, even though it would be highly unusual for one to be in the area.

The September 15, 1977, edition of the *Davis News Journal* reported "Big Foot in the Uintas of Utah: Nothing Conclusive."

The article, by reporter Gary R. Blodgett, stated that parties had been searching the mountains for three weeks and had still not discovered any signs of the creature.

Jerry Dahlberg, a conservation officer with the Utah Division of Wildlife Resources, reported that his team had covered about ten square miles during their search, but had found nothing. Dahlberg did note the remote nature of the area, stating that some of it was "so primitive it looked like it had never before been penetrated by man. We covered the entire Cuberant Basin area one day and the following day searched the Bear River side of the area."

Despite not finding any evidence, Dahlberg wasn't completely dismissing the reports. He told the *Journal*:

"If such a creature is in the area, he would be constantly on the move, but we should be able to find some evidence of existence, such as animal carcasses, torn tree bark, a form of shelter, etc. But we found none."

The officer told the paper that he planned another search around Holiday Park on the Upper Weber River. Dahlberg noted that the area consisted of "miles of rugged terrain" that few people ever explored.

A man and his wife spotted a Bigfoot in Cache County on October 19, 1977. The man had taken his family into the mountains for a camping and hunting trip. The sighting occurred while the man and his wife were scouting the area for signs of deer. According to the report, the creature stepped out in front of the couple as they were making their way down a ridge line. The witness told BFRO investigator Todd Strong that the creature was between seven and eight feet tall and had reddish-brown hair. It was about twenty yards away from the couple. The creature paused for about ten seconds and looked at the couple. The pair turned to look at each other and when they looked back, the Bigfoot had vanished.

Tracks were found at the campsite the following morning indicating that the creature walked around the family's tent during the night.

In its August 15, 1978, edition, Ogden's *Standard-Examiner* covered some weird occurrences that many believed were Bigfoot related.

The report covered incidents experienced by a pair of men camping in the Uinta Mountains that summer. The men were next to Steel Creek west of China Meadows on July 28, 1978, when they heard what they described as a weird "barking" sound accompanied by screams.

The unsettling sounds were coming from a stand of heavy timber near their location and started at around 5:30 in the morning. One man said the sound was like a "barking jabber" that increased in volume and pitch. The men didn't see the creature making the sounds and, in some ways, this was likely more disturbing.

The second report the paper covered involved a 29-year-old resident of Morgan. The man was in his camper parked at Whitney Reservoir below the Cuberant Basin. At one o'clock in the morning, the man's sister-in-law and a friend heard something tramping in the woods near the trailer. Right after this, something rocked the camper from side to side. The man directed a flashlight beam outside and the sounds immediately stopped.

The camper and truck were sturdy and not easily moved, as the Morgan man clarified to the paper: "The camper is an eight-footer on a three-quarter ton truck and there was absolutely no wind. The night was perfectly still."

Whatever it was remained hidden from view. "I just had that eerie feeling that something was watching us. You just know it," the man told reporters.

Whatever the thing was, it wasn't quite finished with the campers. That night, the man, who was sleeping in a small tent, reported that something had walked around his tent in the night, stopped and slapped it, then walked away.

The sister-in-law reported a similar experience, noting that she was "scared to death."

Bigfoot researcher Ryan Layton received a compelling account from Larry Darley of Clearfield who spotted a creature in the fall of 1979.

Darley and his wife were elk hunting in the Monte Cristo range. They were near Mount Mckinnon in Cache County when they saw something odd. Darley states:

"We were sitting at a water hole at twilight. We were about 50 yards away. We heard a commotion, then smelled something real rank. And there was a big, hairy thing on the edge of the water hole."

Larry's wife was holding a rifle at the time, and she looked at the creature through the scope. "It's a monster, you kill it," she said, tossing the rifle to her husband.

Darley looked through the scope and saw the creature clearly himself. He reported:

"The face took up almost the whole scope. It looked like a blond ape. The face was mostly hairy, but it had bald spots and sharp teeth. There was a real wild look in its eyes."

The hunter watched the beast through the rifle's scope for a few moments. As he was watching it, the thing turned its head and looked straight at him as if it sensed it was being observed.

The Darleys ran to their vehicle in a panic and left the area as quickly as possible.

Darley is still puzzled by the incident and has never been able to explain why he didn't fire when he had the beast in his sights.

"That's probably the most scared I've ever been in my life, but there wasn't any reason for it. It didn't do anything but look at me; I guess it just had such a wild expression and bared its teeth, but I don't know if it was threatening or if that was its natural expression."

Ogden Valley

1980s

Bigfoot was very active in the Beehive State in the 1980s. One of the creature's favorite haunts was the Cold Springs Trout Farm in North Ogden. The spot may have been targeted by the creature due to the easy meal it could find by dipping into the ponds of fish. The farm's owner reported that he had been losing fish for years and that, on many occasions, he would find partially eaten fish strewn about the property. An unusual, foul smell (not from the fish) was also frequently present.

Jay Barker, who had reported his group's Bigfoot sighting the previous decade, was working at the fish farm in 1980. On an early spring morning, he was feeding the fish at a pond on the east side of the property when he noticed fish on the lawn around the water. Investigating further, he discovered dozens of dead trout, some intact, but other missing their heads. As he searched the area further, Barker also found large, human shaped footprints in the mud near the pond.

The *North Ogden Connection* looked back on Jay Barker's sightings in its November 17, 2017, edition and included the following details:

"The tracks measured 14 inches long and the toes curled down into the mud. Barker called Utah Fish and Game and informed them about the tracks. They brought plaster with them to cast a mold of one footprint. It could also be seen where Bigfoot had jumped into the pond and walked around, disturbing the moss on the bottom. Fish and Game took the footprint cast and studied it for quite a while before returning it to Jay."

Apparently, officials had little to say about the print.

Jay Barker's sister-in-law lived near the fish farm during the activity there, and she spotted one of the creatures herself. She said it looked in the window of her trailer, and, due to the trailer's height, the creature had to be eight foot tall to peer in like it did. She said the beast had red eyes.

Sometime in the early 1980s, Lee Fielding of Hooper, Weber County, was camping in the Elizabeth Mountain area of the Uintas when something went through his camp and frightened his horses.

Fielding, a Utah Wildlife Resources employee, didn't see the source of the disturbance, but the following day, his horse refused to move in a particular direction. Fielding ran into a group of hunters who had a camp nearby and they told him they had seen a Bigfoot (*Deseret News* June 24, 2009).

Utah researcher Ryan Layton received a report from a man living in Lapoint, Uintah County, who said that, in 1980, he was flying a small plane from Ogden to his home when he spotted a Bigfoot moving across the terrain. It was winter and the man was flying over the High Uintas when he spotted the large, hairy creature walking through deep snow.

The February 12, 1980, edition of the *Deseret News* ran a headline that announced, "2 Report Bigfoot Sightings in South Weber."

Residents of the Davis County town said the hairy creature was wandering around near homes and no one was sure what to make of it.

Paulene Markham was home alone on February 3 when she saw the creature walking along a ridge on a hill behind her house. The paper reports:

"Miss Markham said she was about a half mile from it. She was standing at her kitchen sink, getting a drink of water about 4 p.m., when she looked up and saw it on the hill.

"'I looked at it and I thought, 'Well, I'm going crazy,' she said. 'Then, I walked away from the window and came back, and it was still there.' Miss Markham said she was frightened and curious, but she didn't go outside to get a closer look."

The paper notes that even if Markham wanted to get closer, it would have taken a snowmobile to access the spot.

After the sighting, Markham left for church. Initially, she told one friend about the incident, but no one else.

As it turned out, someone else soon spotted the creature. Ron J. Smith saw the thing in a pasture behind his home the night after the Markham sighting. The man had gone outside to feed his horse when he heard crunching in the snow behind his home. He initially thought it was a prowler or perhaps a teenager up to no good. Scanning the area, he saw the figure about 150 feet away. He focused on it, trying to determine who or what it was. The paper reported Smith's account:

"When he saw the creature in the moonlight, his first thought was that it was a husky high school kid wearing a big coat. He said it walked rapidly across the pasture into a clump of trees. Only then, Smith said, did he become alarmed, because from the trees he heard four loud, inhuman screams in rapid succession. The sounds were something like the cries of a cougar, but louder, Smith said. He said the sounds then stopped for a moment, and by this time he was inside his house. From inside, he heard another three screams, then silence."

Smith waited for a time, then went back outside to check on his horse. He found the animal, uninjured but standing close to the house, looking in the direction of the trees where the creature had gone into the woods.

Smith told his wife about the incident, but she hadn't heard the screams herself.

"I got inside. I told my wife, 'I think it's Bigfoot out there,' I was sort of kidding, but those screams were unbelievable."

Smith was puzzled by the incident and looked around the area the next day to see if there were any tracks. He found something. Tracks that were about a foot and a half long and eight to nine feet apart. There were also impressions of toes, but the horse had trampled the tracks during the night, making it difficult to tell exactly what the creature was.

He spoke with neighbors to find out if they had noticed anything unusual but none of them had anything to report.

While the horse did stick close to the house, Smith said he hadn't noticed any unusual behavior from the animal that night. He did note, however, that the horse had refused to go near the trees for several days prior to the incident and would only eat in a clearing.

Both Markham and Smith stated that the creature, whatever it was, walked like a human but with a much longer stride.

Markham estimated that the thing was between eight and ten feet tall. She said it had long arms and was black or dark brown in color.

It's important to mention that neither Markham nor Smith specifically said they had seen a Bigfoot. Both the witnesses were puzzled by the creature and simply weren't sure what exactly it was.

John Harrington, reporter with the *Ogden Standard-Examiner*, also covered the South Weber sightings in the paper's February 12, 1980, edition.

Harrington wrote that the community was quietly buzzing about the hairy creature after the reported sightings and said that he had seen the tracks himself.

The beast was sighted by at least two people. Its possible tracks were found by a Bigfoot researcher and *Standard-Examiner* reporter John Harrington on Monday.

Harrington states that he wouldn't have believed the accounts, but apparently seeing is believing. "I've never seen tracks like these before!" the reporter exclaimed.

Harrington's report in the paper details the find:

"Jay Barker and I spent Monday afternoon searching for tracks along the canal banks near the area of the Markham sighting. We were ready to call it a day when a line of tracks became visible in the unmelted snow along the dirt road next to the canal. They measured over 15 inches, had clear markings of toes, and appeared to be human, with one exception: the bottom of the feet must have had pads. They were also made by something unusually heavy."

The tracks were about four feet apart and next to the initial find, the men discovered a second set of prints. These were smaller in size but identical in form, indicating that a pair of creatures had passed through the area. Harrington reports that they followed the tracks until the snow ran out.

In his book *South Weber: The Autobiography of One Utah Community*, author Lee Bell notes a curious footnote to the sightings. Around the same time that Markham and Smith saw the creature, another man in South Weber lost a five-year-old horse. Something reportedly frightened the animal so badly that it ran through two barbed wire fences and dropped dead on South Weber Road.

The February 15, 1980, edition of the *Standard-Examiner* reported on some potential physical evidence of Bigfoot—hair samples to be exact.

According to the paper, Paul Woodbury of the Utah Division of Wildlife Resources had the samples found in the area by two Ogden men, Michael Sanders and Steve Ukena. The hair samples were found on a barbed wire fence where it was believed the creature had passed.

The following day, the paper reported on Woodbury's findings announcing them with the headline, "That's Not Hair from 'Bigfoot' Left by Cow."

The wildlife specialist was confident that the hair samples were from "some breed of cattle."

The results were disappointing for Bigfoot researchers in the area, but the search—and sightings—continued, and the creature lingered in the area.

Walter G. Ray of South Weber Drive reported a weird incident at his home. Ray's wife, Myrna, burned a heavy kettle of stew, so she set it on the back porch of the home to cool. During the night, something took the pan to a garden at the back of the property, about 300 yards from the porch, and licked it clean.

Ray probably assumed common animals were responsible, but when Michael Sanders and Steve Ukena showed up at his house, he had to rethink the incident. The trackers had followed Bigfoot's trail to the Ray household.

"I didn't think much about it until these fellows came Wednesday and we went back out to the garden and looked at the tracks around where the pan had been found. It was then I noticed they looked like large bear tracks with pads on the foot."

Other people in the area reported unusual sounds and foul odors. Annette Gardner said she and her husband noticed an odor "like something was dead," and their dogs barked through the night.

In short order, monster hunters from around the county converged on the community in search of the beast. Pickup trucks of armed men were patrolling up and down South Weber

Road looking for any signs of the creature.

The February 27, 1980, edition of the *Ogden Standard Examiner* reported that a Clearfield man named Lee Padilla had a late-night encounter on Riverdale Road. Padilla was traveling east at around 3:30 a.m. when a creature darted across the road twenty-five feet in front of his vehicle.

Padilla was about a mile west of the Weber River when the large, bipedal creature came into view, illuminated by the vehicle's headlights.

Padilla said the thing was between ten and eleven feet tall and hairy. It had long legs, long arms, and brown hair.

"I would say it would weigh about 600 pounds. It crossed the road from north to south and I would estimate it was running about 35 miles an hour. I saw it for maybe four or five seconds."

Padilla says he wasn't frightened by the encounter and was more curious than anything else. He reports that the creature paid no attention to him or his vehicle.

The creature turned down a small, dirt side road. Padilla attempted to follow the beast and put his hi-beams on, turning to direct them toward the creature's path through a field. He didn't spot the thing again, but he did attract the attention of a state highway patrolman who stopped to ask what he was doing.

Padilla told the officer what he had seen after which the patrolman "took off in a hurry." Padilla had the impression that the officer was going to look for the creature himself.

The area was later searched for any signs of the creature's presence, but the ground was so hard packed that no prints were visible.

In April 1980 a thirteen-year-old girl spotted a Sasquatch in Washington Terrace, Weber County. The hairy creature was only about ten feet away, standing with its back to the witness. The thing was in a gully near the Weber River when the girl spotted it. She also reported a foul odor around the area. Frightened by the sight, the girl rushed home. At the same time, the girl's brother was out cutting oak brush in the area and reported that he saw a large, black creature. The report was published in the June 24, 2009, edition of the *Deseret News* in a roundup of Bigfoot sightings in the state.

The May 1, 1980, edition of the *Deseret News* reported on possible Bigfoot tracks found in a residential area of North Ogden.

The tracks were discovered by a homeowner out doing some chores in his yard. The prints were measured at 13 inches in length and 4 inches in width. The homeowner reported being awakened early one morning by screams but was unsure of the source.

Officers from the Utah Division of Wildlife Resources showed up and cast two of the footprints, hoping to study them to determine what the creature was.

Also, in May 1980 a couple from Ogden were picking asparagus along the Weber River near 12th Street and I-15 when they spotted a creature with glowing red eyes. The thing was about 40 yards from their position. The witnesses said the beast was approximately eight feet tall. (*Sasq-Wasatch* website).

Reportedly, the police chief of Garland, Box Elder County, witnessed a Bigfoot when one of the creatures ran in front of his vehicle in 1981. Around the same time, area residents were reporting sightings and track finds (*Deseret News* June 24, 2009).

This incident is especially intriguing since it involves a direct sighting by a law enforcement officer. For a long time, there was no additional information, but the *Utah Bigfoot Blog* received an email about the incident after it repeated the news item. The site's November 1, 2011, update on the story quotes an email the site administrator received about the story involving the police chief:

"[The Police Chief of Garland] had received a call from a farmer on the west edge of Garland on Canal Road one evening that something was scaring his cows. The officer responded and drove along the canal with his light shining from his patrol car, shining it into the canal. About ¼ mile down the road, he saw something that he could not explain. I know he didn't talk about what he saw with too many people. My dad was friends with him, and he shared the experience with my dad after he retired. [The police chief said] 'All I know is, it wasn't human; I saw what I saw.'"

The blog posting spurred a number of other responses including one from DeAnn Sagez who wrote:

"I am the daughter of the police officer who saw big foot. Him, and my 12-year-old niece saw him running across the RR tracks on west factory. It was very real and scared them both a lot. A lot of others in the Garland area saw him around the same time."

According to the March 5, 1981, edition of the *Pleasant Grove Review*, Leonard Howlett and his son Lester, both from Pleasant Grove, discovered footprints in the High Uintas in January that they believed were left by Bigfoot.

The tracks were found in early January at the Howlett's logging camp. According to the paper, prior to the track find, Howlett didn't believe in the existence of the unknown creature:

"Howlett said he has always scoffed at reports of 'Big Foot' or 'Sasquatch,' as the legendary creature is often called. He explained that he has been a logger or a cowboy in the region for many years and had never seen anything that could be construed as 'Big Foot.' That is, until the huge prints were located recently."

Howlett said there were two sets of tracks about six feet apart. He was positive they hadn't been left by bear, mountain lion, or any other known animal in the mountains.

The prints were measured at nineteen inches from heel to the tip of the toe and eleven inches in width at the widest point. The creature's stride was fifty-four inches. Various features of the foot, including toes, instep, and ball of the foot, were clearly visible in some of the prints.

Howlett said he also found a beaver carcass in the area that had been picked clean. There were also strange sounds heard around the camp:

"During the evening before the first prints were found,

there was a sound of crashing in the willows, a sound of something being beaten, and a grunt or a growl."

Writing on the *Sasq-Wasatch* website, Lynn Arave reports a couple of 1983 sightings, one involving a jogger who spotted a Bigfoot early one morning. The creature was near the city cemetery.

The second report from that year came from a group of men who had spotted a creature with glowing red eyes in Wheeler Canyon near the Snow Basin Ski Resort. The men hurriedly left the area after spotting the beast.

Arave also notes that in the mid-1980s, a Roy tire store owner named Bob Taylor saw a Bigfoot. Taylor was bow hunting in Scare Canyon east of the Ogden Valley when he saw the thing. The creature easily stepped over wire fencing. "It's undeniable to me. I saw what I saw…I've never seen anything like it," Taylor stated.

The September 22, 1982, edition of the *Vernal Express* reported on possible Bigfoot activity in the High Uintas. Campers at King's Peak reported that something was tossing large rocks into Kidney Lake at three o'clock in the morning. The reporting witnesses spoke with other campers in the area the following day and they were told that such incidents were common in the region.

Several sources, including Ray Crowe's *Bigfoot Behavior Volume II*, cover the story of Val Kapp who had a strange encounter in Weber County.

Kapp was deer hunting in the Wasatch Mountains in October 1987. He was in the Cache National Forest and was 4-5 miles from the Pineview Reservoir at Magpie Campground.

Arriving around 10 a.m., Kapp found that there were no other campers in the area he had selected. He parked his vehicle and trekked out, crossing a bridge over the south fork of the Ogden River, and following a trail east. The trail eventually forked, and Kapp followed it south through a small canyon. The trail soon turned west, and that's when things got strange for Kapp. He describes the incident:

Cache National Forest

"Not long after I made this turn, I heard this noise. It was a noise that I had never heard before. I just could not believe the lung capacity this thing had. The noise was immense, a low grunting sort of growling type of noise. But what was amazing to me about it was the immense volume of the sound. I could almost feel the volume. I'm not sure if I can put the sound into words, but it was something like 'huuuuuuurrrrruuu.' The sound was a low-pitched sound, but it would drop off even lower at the end. I stopped immediately in my tracks and scanned the slope to my right, which was where the sound had come from."

The sound kept repeating though Kapp was unable to locate the source. He continued moving slowly up the trail, alert and on guard for whatever was making the sound.

Further up the trail, he was able to determine that the noise was coming from behind some trees 350 to 400 feet up a steep slope in front of him. Now that he knew where the animal was, Kapp started making noise, thinking it would frighten the beast away.

The creature, whatever it was, did not leave its position. Kapp sat down on a branch beneath the spot where the animal was hiding. This seemed to agitate the thing and the trees above started shaking.

"I just knew that I was being watched, and whatever was watching me did not want me there. The noise started to intensify...I just could not believe the lung capacity this thing had.

"I really became unnerved when two rocks, about the size of basketballs, came rolling out of the thick cover, down towards me. That's all I needed. I got back up and immediately headed out the way I had come."

Kapp reports that he spent years hunting and fishing alone and never experienced anything like the incident that day in the Wasatch Mountains.

Several reports mention that ranchers near Garland saw a pair of Bigfoots near their lambing pens in February 1988. The creatures showed up after dark. The following day, numerous tracks were found in the area. The report is intriguing, but I have been unable to locate the original source or any witness names for additional follow-up.

1990s

A Utah family traveling at night on a highway near Orangeville in Emery County had to slam on the brakes to avoid hitting a Bigfoot that was standing in the middle of the highway. It remained in place for several minutes and was thirty to forty feet in front of their vehicle. The creature was illuminated by the truck's headlights and after a few moments, it finally moved out of the way (*Deseret News* June 7, 1997).

Bigfoot researcher Thom Cantrall received an account from a man who spotted a Bigfoot in Butterfield Canyon in the early 1990s.

It was late summer, and the witness and his son-in-law were scouting for elk. They walked up the canyon and up a gulch that eventually came to a split. The pair separated with the man taking the northern path and his son-in-law taking the southern route.

About twenty minutes later, the reporting witness was watching a clearing and saw movement in some trees on the far side. He lay quietly watching the area, expecting to see a doe emerge. Instead, he got a surprise. As he told Cantrall:

"Very suddenly, the dark shape darted from the cover it had been in while hiding from me and entered an even thicker, darker copse beyond. It was a large being...running on its hind legs...at least seven feet tall and possibly as much as seven and a half feet. It was massively built and very dark."

Right after the creature moved by, the man's son-in-law emerged from another direction, moments too late to witness the creature himself.

A search of the area did not yield any track discoveries and the men left the area and returned home.

The *Utah Bigfoot Blog* has an account from a woman who saw a creature on a hill at the mouth of Parley's Canyon in 1992.

The woman and her husband were traveling eastbound on I-80 approaching the ramp for I-215 south when her husband pointed out a figure on the side of the hill. They pulled off the road to get a better look at the unusual sight.

Once they had pulled over, they noticed several other vehicles that had done the same with several people gazing up at the figure trying to determine what it was. The witness reports:

"It looked like something big. Usually people don't walk up here, there's no houses or anything.

"It was winter because we thought it looked like it had a snowsuit on. It was really cold. We didn't want to be outside looking at this thing. Back then there was a ton of snow. That's another thing why it was weird. Why would anyone be on that steep of a hill in the winter?"

They watched the figure for about ten minutes. During that time, it walked back and forth and occasionally sat down on a large rock.

The figure was dark in color and the woman said, "We could see it easily against the white of the snow. It was walking on such a steep hill. It wasn't easy to do but it didn't look like it was struggling."

The *OregonBigfoot.com* website contains a report about a December 7, 1992, sighting in City Creek Canyon in Salt Lake County. The sighting took place about a mile northeast of the state capital building in Salt Lake City.

The reporting witness was at work and spotted something crawling through underbrush on a nearby hill. The witness reported:

"I'm new to Utah and my first thought was it was a wild animal, a bear. But the animal I saw came out of the underbrush and stood up. Without any misstep it walked upright at an angle up the hill, which at my best guess would be about a 45-degree angle. With approximately 12 inches of snow—there was no slipping, no struggling and with no effort the animal walked up the hill to a cave-like opening. It ducked its head and walked in."

As the event was unfolding, two of the witness's co-workers came in and also observed the figure. One suggested it was a surveyor at work, but the reporting witness pointed out that if that were the case, he would have been wearing his bright orange vest.

"They said, 'I don't know...must be something' and walked away. Surprised that they acted like it was nothing, I continued to watch as the animal walked out of the opening a little downhill, then suddenly it stopped and it looked right up at me and with a sharp jerk down motion of its head, it walked quickly up the hill to a small rock outcropping and ducked out of view."

Philip Rife's *Bigfoot Across America* contains a 1994 report involving a group of boy scouts who encountered a Bigfoot near Baker Lake summit in Summit County. The creature was spotted during a nighttime trek. The reporting witness stated:

"We were walking down a trail at night. It was a full moon. There was a stream, and on the other side I saw a hominid. It was walking on two feet. Not a bear, not a gorilla, not a chimp, not any ape I've ever seen. I'm very, very sure on that."

The creature was reportedly dark in color, between six and seven feet in height, and was stout and fit. The witness also noticed that the beast had a "high crown" and moved with a twist at its hips.

Utah researcher Dave Rosenfeld received an interesting report about a 1994 sighting at Moon Lake in the Uintas.

The reporting witness and a friend were walking down Brown Duck Trail when they heard a "low, grunting-like bark." Although the sound was unusual, they dismissed it and continued their trek down the trail. They continued to hear the sound every five to ten minutes and suddenly felt as if they were being watched.

The sound of a limb snapping alerted the witness who quickly looked in the direction of the sound. He told Rosenfeld:

"As I looked into the thick pines where the sound came

from, I saw two dark, hairy, head and shoulders moving quickly away at about 40-50 feet away."

Uinta Mountains

The creatures vanished into the trees and were only in view for approximately five seconds. Despite the quick view, the witness was confident that it was something unusual:

"Now, being that close I was certain it wasn't human, or a couple of bears. One was smaller than the other. They were quite silent while they were moving, except for the one loud snap."

The man said that he never saw the creatures' faces but said that their hair was reddish brown in color and long. The upper torsos were described as muscular.

A BFRO report details a sighting from May 19, 1994, in Garfield County. A man named Bob and a companion were hiking in the Escalante Wilderness and were on a bench headed toward Deer Creek, their planned campsite.

The sun was directly overhead, and the pair were walking in a westerly direction when Bob spotted movement on the top of the rise ahead. The witness describes the figure:

"Though this had a human shape, it was too large, and it was white—I mean paper white, not Caucasian. The creature appeared to be pacing as it looked for something.

"Suddenly I became very aware it had spotted us as it ducked behind the rocky outcroppings and was obscured from our view. As we were hiking toward the area to cross the bench, we observed, as we got closer, that the area where the creature stood was on the highest point and would require all of our climbing skills to reach."

Unsure if the creature was dangerous or not, the hikers decided against trying to reach the point and continued along their route. Apparently, the creature was still up on the peak as Bob soon realized:

"About half of a mile down the westward slope we both had that feeling we were being watched. We both turned and looked up to that area where we had previously sighted the creature and it was watching us again—then quickly ducked down so we could not see it."

In a follow-up interview with a BFRO investigator, Bob added a few additional notes. He reported that the creature was between seven and nine feet tall and initially had one of its arms up to shield its eyes. Bob has always been unsure exactly what the beast was and states:

"It was some sort of humanoid, too big and too agile to be human. I guess I could accept Sasquatch; it walked on two legs."

It's also notable that *Outside Magazine* refers to the area of the sighting as "the most wild and remote place in the contiguous U.S."

The *Sasq-Wasatch* website contains a report from 1996 involving a witness listed as "Jeri" of Eden, Utah. Jeri claims to have driven through a "herd" of Bigfoot as she was traveling late one night through Ogden Valley. The "herd" was somewhere near the Shanghai Canyon area. Take it for what you will.

The same site also notes a spring 1996 account involving a group of children in North Ogden's Coldwater Canyon who were chased by a Bigfoot.

A lone hiker saw a Bigfoot in 1996

A hiker in Utah County had a daylight sighting of a Bigfoot in May 1996. The witness was in the Wasatch Mountains above the town of Pleasant Grove and spotted the creature just after entering Grove Creek Canyon. According to the witness's statement on the BFRO website:

"I saw a large red animal up on the rim of the canyon, about 100 feet above me. It looked about as tall as a large man. There was a little wind, but I did not notice any strange smell. I quickly realized that I was looking at a Bigfoot. I stood and observed the animal for about 5 seconds, then it walked away from the rim of the canyon, out of view."

The hiker spotted the creature between three and four p.m. and found no further evidence of the creature.

A report on *Oregonbigfoot.com* relates a sighting from June 1, 1996, that took place in the Escalante Monument, Garfield County. It was early afternoon, and the witnesses apparently surprised the creature. The report states:

"Its behavior and reaction were completely human. It was scouting for something to the north and when it saw us, it ducked behind a rock to avoid being observed. Because we didn't realize what it was, and thought its behavior was odd— anyone that far out in the wilderness would have been pleased to see us instead of hiding—we decided not to investigate at that time. We did not want to put ourselves in danger."

Cautious, but still needing to reach the other side, the hikers circled around so they could head down. While doing so, they noticed the creature watching them.

Two days later, the witnesses made a return visit to inspect the site and looked closely at the area where they had spotted the creature coming and going. They were shocked to realize that the rocks the thing was peering over were much larger than expected. The witnesses dubbed the area "the fortress" because of how protected it was. The rock formations were found to be between 65-70 inches high. One witness stated:

"This seemed incredible to me because I was able to clearly see the creature from below while it was pacing within the fortress, and it raised its leg and placed its foot on one of the formations as it peered north. This means that the height of the creature had to be at least 12 ft. tall to accommodate these movements."

A driver traveling on Highway 89 in Garfield County near Panguitch saw a Bigfoot at around seven or eight in the evening one fall night in 1997. The witness reported to the BFRO:

"I was about halfway thru Circleville Canyon when just at the edge of my headlights I saw something big on the edge of the road. I started to slow down, didn't want to hit it should it run in front of me. But as I got closer, it stood up and I thought for a second it was a person. Then it started running. It ran across the road approximately 70 feet in front of my car. My heart was pounding. It was huge and hairy with long arms. It ran sort of bent over, but very quickly. But not human like, as it didn't bounce. It disappeared into the dark on the other side of the highway. I was far too scared to stop and see if there were any tracks or anything."

In a follow-up interview with investigator TF Zamiski, the woman said the creature was over seven feet tall, had no neck, and was built "like a pro wrestler." She also commented that it had a gait that was "smooth and not bouncy like a human."

A report on the *Bigfoot Encounters* website involves an incident that took place in Emigration Canyon in the Wasatch Mountains in 1998. Four people went out around ten o'clock at night to do some mud driving. The group had stopped on the side of the road to make some adjustments to the truck. The group noticed that one of its members was "frozen stiff" and staring at something. The others soon realized what was so compelling—a Bigfoot was standing about ten feet in front of the vehicle.

The creature stood swaying from left to right staring at the group. They got back in the vehicle and blew the horn, hoping to scare the creature away, but the action had the opposite effect. The Bigfoot started moving toward the truck.

The group became so frightened that the driver threw the vehicle in reverse and slammed the gas, backing away from the beast as quickly as possible.

The creature turned and went off the road, up a slope, and into the woods where it disappeared in seconds.

Bigfoot researcher Dave Carver received an account from a witness who saw a Bigfoot in Ogden Canyon in 1999.

The witness, Gina, says it was either March or April at around two in the morning when she spotted the creature. She was on her way home and was driving slowly because she was traveling through heavy rain.

She spotted what she first thought was a man walking toward her about 30 yards before Perry's Camp Bridge. She told Carver:

"My first thought was 'why would a guy be wearing a fur coat in the middle of a rainstorm?' I actually had to swerve to miss hitting it. It didn't move out of the way. As I passed by this thing, I realized it wasn't a man in a coat as it was way too big and bulky to be a man. I know it was not a man or a moose or anything like that. I know exactly what it was."

A man and his son out on an ATV ride in the fall of 1999 spotted a Bigfoot around dusk. It was sometime in late September and the pair were in the mountains above Huntsville in Cache County. They were spending a week camping, and the incident occurred on the fifth day of their trip. The father was driving the four-wheeler and they rode for some time, finally turning around in what appeared to be an old camp. The witness told the BFRO:

"It was turning dusk. We made the turn and started to move back onto the road when my son tapped me on the shoulder and told me to go faster. I turned to look at what he saw and could not believe my eyes. There about fifty feet or so away was a large upright creature casually strolling in a parallel line with us. He was about seven or eight feet tall with a stride that I cannot forget. He moved smoothly along an old fence line where he turned into the woods and disappeared. He was dark in color and didn't seem to be coming after us."

In a follow-up report, the witness said the creature was between seven and eight feet tall and dark in color. He described it as broad but "not overly huge," with long hair on its head. The head was described as "blocky," and the creature leaned forward slightly.

The pair continued their camping trip but had no further incidents during their time in the area.

2000s

A man camping in Summit County near the Utah/ Wyoming border had a late-night sighting of a Bigfoot on the night of June 12-13, 2001. The man was camping with some family and friends when the weather turned cold, forcing the group to sleep in a vehicle.

"Sometime between 11 p.m. and 2 a.m., I was awakened by the feeling that I was being watched. I looked to my right to find out if I could see anything, but I was unable to, so I tried to go back to sleep. However, I could not shake the feeling that I was being watched and when I opened my eyes I looked out into the meadow in front of the Suburban and saw a creature I believe to have been a Bigfoot. It was walking upright heading north through the meadow. I would guess its height to have been between 6.5 to 7 feet."

The witness told a BFRO investigator that the creature was between 75 and 100 yards away when he spotted it.

A man and his girlfriend were on a camping and fishing

trip in Beaver County in August 2001 when they encountered a Bigfoot at their fishing spot.

The witness says they were in Fish Lake National Forest and had chosen a time in August during the middle of the week in order to escape the crowds. They enjoyed a couple of days of solitude until an incident on Wednesday morning.

The reporting witness was standing at the water's edge casting a fishing line when he saw what he first thought was a bear drinking from the lake. The man pointed the creature out to his girlfriend and suddenly the "bear" stood upright on two legs. The man told the BFRO:

"I've never been so scared in my life, though I didn't feel threatened. What we observed was something walking like a human, covered with dark brown hair. It was moving back in the woods. It didn't seem to notice us, or it didn't care we were there. I am convinced what we saw was a Bigfoot. There is no other animal like the animal or thing we saw that day. I didn't investigate afterward. We headed back to camp to pack and go home. We are now back to camping 4th of July at state run campgrounds."

In a follow-up interview, the man clarified that the creature was about 200 yards from his location and had a muscular, athletic build.

A couple driving on Highway 91 in southern Utah's Washington County saw a Bigfoot near the Shivwits Indian Reservation on February 13, 2002.

"He came up from the south by the Santa Clara River. We saw him in our headlights. He was about in the middle of the road when we saw him. He was swinging his arms like a human, and he kept glancing back to see how fast we were approaching. He was 8 to 10 feet tall, had a hairy body, and looked like the ones I have seen on TV. His hair was brown in color."

The reporting witness was in the passenger seat of the vehicle and said that the driver slowed down to about 25 mph and that they watched the Bigfoot as it was illuminated by the headlights. It was approximately seven o'clock in the evening and the creature was about four car lengths away.

BFRO investigator Todd Strong spoke with the woman and learned that the Bigfoot approached the road from the left, having come up out of the river bottoms. It moved across the road and looked at the vehicle several times as if trying to determine if it was in danger of being struck.

The Western Bigfoot Society received a report that a gray/brown Bigfoot was spotted in November 2002 around the Lagoon Amusement Park in Farmington. Reportedly, area residents also reported weird screams at night.

A Bigfoot was reportedly wandering along a canal behind some houses in North Logan, Cache County, in 2003. According to the report on the *Earthfiles* website, the witness belongs to a family who have seen the creatures multiple times. According to the report:

"The mother first saw a Bigfoot when she was 15 years old in 1968 in almost the same place where her 16-year-old son saw another large, hairy creature on January 2, 2003. It was 11:30 p.m."

Lynn Arave mentions a May 2003 report involving a group of teenagers: Chad Ellis, Zac Morby, Porter Perkins, Doug Steenblik, and Nate Kennaley. The boys were residents of Farmington who heard strange sounds along the Lagoon Trail just east of the Lagoon Amusement Park. The boys also noticed a foul odor in the area. More significantly, they spotted what they believed to be the source of the stench and noises—a tall, grayish brown creature that lurked among the trees.

Other Farmington residents also reported odd noises in the area that couldn't be attributed to any known animal.

A Farmington resident named Julie told me that she'd had an encounter on the same trail in 2004. She was eighteen at the time and she and a friend were walking the trail just as the sun was going down. They heard a noise that sounded "like someone chattering their teeth really fast." The girls stopped to listen, and the sound stopped. They resumed walking and the noise started again. At this point, they expected a teenage boy trying to be scary or funny and they stopped and called out,

"Who's there?" There was no answer, but Julie's friend noticed some movement among nearby trees. Still convinced it was a teenage boy, the girls started to move toward the trees. The witness told me:

"We took maybe three steps and then it stepped out. It was about seven feet tall and looked like a gorilla with black hair with some gray in it. We both screamed and took off running, not even looking back. We never walked that trail again."

Two men hunting in Summit County in the fall of 2004 surprised a Bigfoot near Chalk Creek. One of the men reported the incident to the BFRO, stating:

"We were climbing up out of a small draw onto a flat meadow. As we got to the top of it, we both saw something very black in color move into a small stand of pine trees. It let out a huge whoooff sort of sound as it went in. Also, it moved a pine bow that flipped from the ground to about five feet in the air."

The creature was only about thirty feet from the men, and the reporting witness believes that they surprised the thing, leading it to act in an aggressive manner.

"We backed up, and this thing let out a low, guttural growl at us. You could hear its teeth chatter also. I have felt fear in my life, but a sense of evil came over me."

In later conversation, investigator Todd Strong discovered that the reporting witness had worked as a licensed hunting guide and wildlife artist. As a result, he was very familiar with the region's wildlife.

The man told Strong that the creature had jet black hair, not fur, and that it was about nine feet tall.

A family traveling northwest of Vernal in Uintah County on December 25, 2004, watched a Bigfoot cross the road in front of their SUV.

"C.H." reported the incident to the BFRO and stated that his wife was driving the vehicle and that both she and the couple's daughter also saw the creature. It was first seen stepping over a wire fence about 40' from the road.

Investigator TF Zamiski reported the man's description of

the beast:

"The face of this 7' tall plus animal was bordered with hair. The face was basically flat, unlike a gorilla. It had dark eyes, a prominent brow, a nose with flared nostrils. The mouth was wide and slightly open. The skin on the body that was visible was lighter in color than the fur. Its head was peaked, but not pointed, with no apparent ears. It had a definite chin and a very thick neck."

The witness also reported that the Bigfoot's hair was charcoal gray in color. It crossed the road and headed up a steep embankment, using its arms like legs, knuckle down gorilla style, to move over the terrain.

The family returned to a relative's house in Dry Fork Canyon and told others about the sighting. The man's sister spoke to neighbors about the incident, and several of them told her there had been additional sightings in the area.

A Tooele County report on the BFRO site comes from a man who spotted a "monkey-looking thing" outside his window in the summer of either 2004 or 2005.

The reporting witness, a young man, says that he and his mother both witnessed the creature in an empty field behind their home in the Oquirrh Mountains.

"It was about 100 yards away. It was jogging toward the mountains east of where I was. It was black and looked like it had short fur. It wasn't very tall. Maybe four feet. It kind of ran like a monkey. You know how monkeys run on their hands sort of crouched over. I watched for about a minute until it went down into a ditch."

A man driving a snowplow on January 5, 2005, watched a Bigfoot cross the road in front of his truck. The witness told the BFRO that he was plowing snow in Cache County on US 89 between 12:30 and 1:00 a.m. He was near the Franklin Basin Road when he spotted something ahead which prompted him to flip on the truck's plow lights. The bright lights illuminated a creature, about seven feet in height, walking across the road. The witness reported that the creature turned and looked at him but continued to walk across the highway and was quickly out of view. His report adds the additional notation:

The Oquirrh Mountains

"That morning I heard on the radio of someone reporting a sighting up Cub River in Idaho. The areas are connected by the Franklin Basin Road which runs from Logan Canyon to Cub River."

The witness is confident that what he saw was not a man.

In mid-September 2005 a man and his wife out enjoying the fall colors in Utah County spotted a Bigfoot running across a small, grassy flat. The couple were at the Sterling Hollow Trailhead by Covered Bridge Canyon at the southeast corner of Maple Mountain. They were initially standing by their jeep looking out at the view, but the woman felt uneasy and wanted to sit in the jeep. The man also felt uncomfortable and started the vehicle. As he turned the key, he spotted a "big, fast black hairy object" to his left. The man turned and watched the creature. It reportedly moved very quickly and covered a lot of ground.

The couple talked and agreed that they had seen a Bigfoot. The woman reported that she had been observing it from the moment she sat down in the jeep.

In an interview with Bigfoot investigator Chad Hamblin, the man provided details of the creature, noting that it had straight, dark brown hair all over its body, including the ears. According to the report:

"The nose was barely visible because of the hair. It had dark lips and you couldn't see the teeth. The head was shaped more like a human head than a gorilla's head. No neck was visible because of the long facial hair. When it moved it looked like it was hunched over, trying to run but stay hidden. Its legs looked different than a bear's legs, with what appeared to be feet rather than paws."

The witness, a long-time hunter, returned to the location later that night with hunting equipment and attempted to locate the creature but was unable to find it.

In September 2006 a woman camping in the Monte Cristo area of Cache County saw a tall, dark humanoid figure twenty-five yards from her. The woman saw the creature in the moonlight and reported that her dog whimpered through the night (*Deseret News* June 24, 2009).

A 2007 account comes from a man out hunting around three in the afternoon in Cache County. The hunter went out to the Wellsville Mountains west of Logan on October 20 and turned off a paved road, going past a home that was under construction.

He walked a short distance, sat down, and proceeded to observe some mule deer that were bedded down in the trees. His observations were disrupted by a loud crashing sound coming from the trees near the construction site. Using a pair of binoculars, the man spotted the source of the noise: a creature that he first thought was a black bear. He quickly realized that the thing was not a bear and was moving in a very fast and graceful manner. As he recounts:

"I watched as it plowed through thick brush like a bull until it made it to more open ground in the trees and I noticed how strange it really was. It was moving on two legs and moving fast. I looked and saw all the deer running."

The witness was terrified at the sight of the creature. He

loaded a bullet into his rifle and quickly backed away from the area, returning to his car and leaving the scene.

The witness was a college student at the time and had been hunting the region from the time he was fourteen. He told the BFRO that he has not returned to the area since he saw the creature.

A trio of young men camping in American Fork Canyon on June 27, 2008, had a series of strange incidents culminating in a Bigfoot sighting.

The trio spent a day doing some fishing and set up camp north of Tibble Fork Lake. In the evening, sitting around their camp, they heard a faint whistling noise. The sound persisted and got closer to their camp. As the sound grew louder, the men noticed a strong, unusual odor in the air.

The reporting witness states that as the group prepared to bed down for the night, he walked about 10 yards away from camp to relieve himself. He saw what he thought was a person walking about 40 yards from his position. This was followed by the sound of a stick hitting a tree two times. His report on the *Bigfoot Encounters* website describes what happened next:

"Whatever you want to call it, but I know what I saw. I saw Sasquatch standing upright walking towards the tree. It was standing at least 7 feet tall, not intimidated by any means. It looked at me or in my direction. My heart was pounding as the whistling noise got louder, very loud. I ran back to camp, telling my friends what I just saw. They believed me, telling me they felt the same way—that is, as if we were being watched."

One of the other men told the witness that earlier in the day he had seen a large figure walking around near their campsite.

The group quickly gathered their things, fled to their vehicle, and left the area.

A man driving west of Flaming Gorge Dam in Daggett County saw a Bigfoot on December 7, 2008.

The witness told the BFRO that he was driving around ten o'clock at night on his way to Vernal. As he went over the Flaming Gorge Pass, he spotted a pair of red eyes 6 ½ to 7 feet up. He hit the brakes and turned to get his headlights on the figure. He reports:

"My first thought was a bear that was standing on its hind legs, but then I noticed it was not a bear. By that time, he turned around and slowly started walking away from me. It had very long, black matted hair and I know for a fact that it wasn't a bear by the way it walked. It scared me so bad I got out of there and I did not care to go back."

On June 10, 2009, Ryan Burns spotted a reddish colored hairy creature in the woods just south of his home in Duchesne in Duchesne County.

Burns is a Utah based researcher who has written about Skinwalker Ranch. He reports that when he first spotted the creature walking on Reservation Ridge, he thought it was a human wearing a fur coat, but he felt strange as he was looking at the figure. Burns says that whatever it was, it turned and looked at him then vanished into the trees. He pursued the thing on horseback, but it escaped. Burns doesn't believe that a human could have eluded him so easily, especially since he was on a horse.

The area is a fairly remote one, though Burns did later speak with some campers who had been in the area the previous week. They said they had spotted a strange figure that disturbed them enough that they left the area.

A man backpacking at Grandaddy Lake in Duchesne County saw a white-haired Bigfoot in the summer of 2009. It was July 11, and the reporting witness, his brother, and four nephews had hiked to the lake and were setting up their campsite. The man's brother had gone to secure the group's food when the witness spotted the creature. The group's camp was near a group of scouts who were also out for a camping trip. The witness reports:

"I glanced over toward where the scouts were when I saw something with long white/blond hair was staring into their camp. It must have been startled by our presence because it took off running extremely fast toward the marsh area. I remember very vividly the hair bouncing as it took long strides. The lack of noise that it made along with the speed startled me to the point that I unbuckled my gun holster, concerned for our safety."

The witness said the creature was about six feet in height. It was standing behind very tall vegetation, so he was not able to see more of the thing before it ran from the scene.

He emphasized during an interview that the thing looked much larger than a human and that it moved much quicker than a man with longer strides.

The witness is an experienced outdoorsman and is very familiar with the wildlife in the Uinta Mountains.

The *Bigfoot Seekers* website reports that Todd Man of Ogden spotted a Bigfoot near the hot water spring at the mouth of Ogden Canyon in April 2011. The sighting took place around 2 a.m.

Man's first thought was that he was seeing an escaped gorilla. The creature was black and silver in color.

Utah Stories Magazine (October 17, 2012) reports on a 2012 incident in the town of Liberty, Weber County. A young man named Sam went out to feed his chickens and noticed a large, shadowy figure nearby.

It was August and there was a full moon and Sam watched as the figure moved into the trees in his neighbor's yard.

At first the boy thought the figure was his neighbor or a prankster, but while observing it, he realized a few things. First, it was very large. Sam reports that he's six feet tall and he estimated that the prowler was about eight feet in height. It was also covered from "head to toe in black."

A crashing sound behind him drew the boy's attention and he turned to see another creature, this one smaller, moving toward the first one.

The smaller figure moved up a gully that winds east to the mountains. Sam told the magazine:

"The creepy thing was that they didn't say anything to each other before the one just took off. Then the big one just stood there staring me down. I was a little scared. I definitely

Was a gorilla on the loose?

picked up on a message from him, like he was saying, 'Don't follow us.'"

A couple of days later, Sam and his mother were in the family garden and discovered that their tomato plants had been picked clean. He also reports that there was a large impression in the grass by their duck pond as if something had reclined or slept there.

The *Sasq-Wasatch* website reports possible sightings along with a discovery of both tracks and handprints in May 2013. The evidence was found on Skyline Trail in the Wasatch Mountains between North Ogden and Ogden Valley. The incident sounds promising, but no further details have been presented.

Ogden resident Todd Man, who had reportedly spotted a Bigfoot in April 2011, reported that he spotted a creature again at the same location—the mouth of Ogden Canyon—in May 2013.

According to a report in the *Ogden Standard Examiner* in its June 23, 2013, edition, Man saw the creature around two a.m. The paper notes that it was Man's second Bigfoot sighting in two years. This time around, Man said there must have been another witness in the area because he heard someone shout "It's a monster." Unfortunately, no other witnesses have ever come forward.

Researcher Ron Johnson received a report from John, a construction worker from Arizona who was working on a remodeling job in Price in 2015. On Sunday, March 8, John was on a dirt road that paralleled the Price River and the Union Pacific Railroad. John and a friend were returning from a visit to the Mounds area in Carbon County when they encountered a large animal standing in the middle of the road. John stopped the vehicle and the pair looked at the creature for a moment. The thing was about seven feet tall and had long, sandy brown hair with black accents.

John blew the truck's horn, and the creature issued a "loud growling type sound," then darted off, running up a hill to the east.

The September 14, 2016, edition of the *Provo Daily Herald*

reported a sighting that occurred west of Provo, Utah County. A family was driving near the airport and one of the children was in the backseat filming the scenery as they passed. The child spotted a large, hairy figure at the edge of a cornfield and asked the family what it was.

The video was taken from the backseat of a moving vehicle, so as expected, the images are too fleeting and unclear to determine what the figure really was.

In recent years, Provo has been a hotspot for purported videos of Bigfoot. Unfortunately, they are often blurry or taken at a great distance, or worse, outright hoaxes.

The Utah Statesman ran a report on October 22, 2021, announcing "Bigfoot Sightings Spike in Northern Utah." The article by Clarissa Casper states:

"For years, Bigfoot believers in Cache Valley say they have felt alone in their experiences. But the coronavirus pandemic—and a Facebook group—has brought together these people with unusual encounters."

Casper spoke with the online group's founder, Jon Marshall, who noted that the group had been receiving an increased number of messages and postings over the fall. Marshall attributed the increase of reports with the increase in campers and hikers exploring the mountains during the fall season.

The reporter also spoke with Nicki Frey, a wildlife specialist from Utah State University. Presented with the question of a possible Bigfoot in the Utah mountains, Frey responded that the reports were likely due to the presence of black bears.

"They are surprisingly humanistic," Frey noted, saying that there was likely a bear den around the reported hotspots—the White Pine and Tony Grove campsites.

However, Frey did not completely dismiss the accounts and stated, "Maybe they are seeing something unique—one never knows."

Bigfoot and the Mormons

In the early 2000s a series of articles and discussions on various online sites whipped up attention for an unusual idea—that the Mormons believed in Bigfoot AND that they knew exactly what the creature was. According to Mormon authorities, Bigfoot was none other than the Biblical Cain, the first murderer.

As outrageous as the theory sounds, it wasn't the first time that the idea had circulated, and the basis of the theory is rooted in a purported encounter from the early 1800s.

Reportedly, in 1835, an early LDS apostle named David W. Patten encountered a bizarre figure while serving on a mission in Tennessee. The account has been published in a number of sources, notably in Spencer W. Kimball's 1969 book *The Miracle of Forgiveness*. Patten's account reads:

"As I was riding along the road on my mule, I suddenly noticed a very strange personage walking beside me for about two miles. His head was about even with my shoulders as I sat in my saddle. He wore no clothing but was covered with hair. His skin was very dark. I asked him where he dwelt and he replied that he had no home, that he was a wanderer in the earth and traveled to and fro. He said he was a very miserable creature, that he had earnestly sought death during his sojourn upon the earth, but that he could not die, and his mission was to destroy the souls of men. About the time he expressed himself thus, I rebuked him in the name of the Lord Jesus Christ and by virtue of the holy priesthood, and commanded him to go hence, and he immediately departed out of my sight."

Kimball's *The Miracle of Forgiveness* became a staple read for Mormons, often recommended to those about to go on missions or those struggling with the concepts of sin.

The author included the story of Patten's encounter in a chapter on unforgivable sins. In discussing murder, the author points to what he calls "an interesting story" about Cain after which he relates the Patten account.

Cain is the biblical figure who killed his brother, Abel, and became the first murderer. Because of his dreadful act, he was "marked." How exactly he was marked isn't specified, and over the years, religious scholars have debated what form the mark took.

In Genesis 4:12 we learn that the Lord told Cain: "a fugitive and a vagabond shalt thou be in the earth." Some interpret this as Cain being cursed to forever wander the earth.

The Bigfoot-Mormon connection got new life with the 2001 publication of *Clan of Cain: The Genesis of Bigfoot*, by Shane Lester. Lester tied in the Patten sighting with the Biblical Nephilim and his novel purportedly revealed "secret truths."

In an article for the Fall 2007 edition of the *Journal of Mormon History*, author Matthew Bowman addresses the topic under the title *A Mormon Bigfoot: David Patten's Cain and the Conception of Evil in LDS Folklore*.

Bowman doesn't think much of Lester's novel or his claim. As his article in the Journal states:

"Lester made the following claim: 'A recently uncovered document reveals a possible connection between the origins of the Mormon Church (Church of Jesus Christ of Latter-Day Saints) and Bigfoot. Searching through the archives of historical church documents, the author, Shane Lester, uncovered an extraordinary story that becomes the foundation of a new theory about the origins of Bigfoot. 'I uncovered an obscure historical document that sheds new light on the Bigfoot mystery. I used this encounter as the basis for a fictional story that links the mystical, legend of Bigfoot to the origins of Mormonism."

Bowman goes on to state that the "obscure document" is anything but obscure, having been previously published in a popular Mormon book (Kimball's *The Miracle of Forgiveness*).

Once one digs into the Patten account, some historical

issues arise. Although the account is from 1835, it seems that Patten himself was not the author of the passage. The encounter first appeared in a biography of Patten published in 1904 by Lycurgus Wilson.

Wilson wrote that the details of the encounter came from a letter written by Abraham Smoot who recalled Patten telling him the tale. This makes the account a third hand one at best, but beyond this, there are other details that don't match.

The recounting of Patten's encounter reportedly came from a letter that Smoot wrote to the President of the Mormon church, Joseph Smith. Unfortunately, the dates don't match. Smith became president of the church in 1901, but Smoot died in 1895 meaning he couldn't have written to President Smith unless he did so from the grave!

We're left to wonder if Smoot fabricated the account, and if so, why? Perhaps some of the facts became jumbled in Wilson's book on Patten but at this point, it's difficult to know the full details of the tale.

Bowman mentions another account that ties into the supposed Bigfoot-Mormon connection. It comes from a 1919 manuscript that describes Hawaiian missionary E. Wesley Smith and his encounter with a strange creature. Smith was reportedly attacked by a "huge, hairy creature" the night before his mission was dedicated. Much like the Patten encounter, Smith was able to drive the thing off by invoking the name of Christ.

Smith's brother, president of the church, told Wesley that the creature attacking him must have been Cain and referred his brother to the Patten account.

Those seeking some kind of Biblical era confirmation of the existence of Bigfoot and how the creature plays into religious belief have also pointed to an account in the apocryphal *Book of Jasher* that they believe adds further weight to the Cain/Bigfoot connection. The passage (Jasher 2:26-30) recounts the death of Cain. The point of interest here is Cain's appearance:

"And Lamech was old and advanced in years, and his eyes were dim that he could not see, and Tubal Cain, his son, was leading him and it was one day that Lamech went into the field and Tubal Cain his son was with him, and whilst they were walking in the field, Cain the son of Adam advanced towards them; for Lamech was very old and could not see much, and Tubal Cain his son was very young. And Tubal Cain told his father to draw his bow, and with the arrows he smote Cain, who was yet far off, and he slew him, for he appeared to them to be an animal. And the arrows entered Cain's body although he was distant from them, and he fell to the ground and died. And the Lord requited Cain's evil according to his wickedness, which he had done to his brother Abel, according to the word of the Lord which he had spoken. And it came to pass when Cain had died, that Lamech and Tubal went to see the animal which they had slain, and they saw, and behold Cain their grandfather was fallen dead upon the earth."

The description of Cain as an animal is a curious one at the least. Unfortunately, no further description is offered and many people who have read the passage jump to the conclusion that Cain was a hair-covered humanoid—a bit of a leap.

Bowman and others believe that the convergence of several folklore aspects in the state came together when the wave of Bigfoot encounters was reported in the 1980s in South Weber.

Even though some modern Mormons do believe that there's some kind of connection between Cain and Bigfoot, most disregard the idea and, of course, the church itself does not take any official stance on the subject.

Bigfoot and the Mormons

PART THREE
Creatures in the Water

For a landlocked state, Utah has some amazing water features. From the unique Great Salt Lake, to recreational, freshwater lakes like Lake Powell and Bear Lake, there are plenty of places to get your aquatic fix in the Beehive State.

Of course, there are also monstrous legends associated with many of these bodies of water. Sometimes, the rumors are scant and undefined or even wrong. Numerous sources list a monster in Utah's Mud Lake but there's a big problem with the tale—the lake doesn't exist! According to Utah's Department of Environmental Quality, there's no record of a "Mud Lake" in the state, nor is there a listing of any such a body of water in Utah in historical documents. The confusion may have arisen from an old news article published in Utah but discussing a Mud Lake monster in another state.

Three Lakes Ranch in Kanab is reportedly the home of a water monster, though sadly, there are no solid accounts or eyewitness reports. The ranch is known for a lost treasure legend that includes a haunted lake so this may simply be a distortion of some of the weird tales associated with the place.

Utah has a lot of treasure legends, from the vast gold hoard of Montezuma, to lost mines and buried outlaw gold, and some of these treasure troves have unusual guardians.

Spirit Lake, high in the Uintas, is one of the possible locations of gold from the lost Rhoades mine. The Rhoades treasure legend dates back to the 1850s when Thomas Rhoades was commissioned by Mormon President Brigham Young to retrieve gold hidden by the Utes at a site called the "Carre Shinob" mines.

The gold horde was purportedly abandoned by the Spanish

in 1776 and only select members of the Ute tribe knew where it was hidden. The gold was difficult to access and well-guarded and Spirit Lake held a monster that helped protect the treasure.

The creature, known appropriately as the Spirit Lake Monster, is described as a serpent-like beast, or something that resembles a dinosaur.

The Gold of Carre-Shinob by Kerry Ross and Lisa Lee Boren contains an interesting account involving the monster from a Ute elder known as "Wash" Wash had important connections in the Ute tribe, as the book tells us:

"Tabuache, or Tab-Wash, was best known as 'Wash.' Wash was related to Timpanogos leader Chief Tabiona. He was a sub-chief under his cousin Chief Walkara. The Timpanogos (usually classified as Ute people) were displaced and sent to the Uintah and Ouray Indian Reservation."

Wash was purportedly one of the few tribal elders who knew the secret location of the Carre-Shinob horde. He claimed that he'd seen the gold while on a fishing trip in the mountains. Seeing glistening in the water, Wash couldn't resist getting one of the bars, but the water was too cold to dive in. The Ute created a makeshift tool with a pole and some wire. Fashioning a loop that he could tighten on one end, the man proceeded to try to fish one of the gold bars out of the water. The task proved challenging, but after many attempts he was finally able to get one of the bars in hand.

According to Ross and Boren, Wash intended to retrieve more of the gold but was deterred:

"Wash told a most unusual story. He said he was about to return to the water for another bar when he heard a strange sound emanating from beneath the ledges at the deepest part of the lake. Looking up, he saw a creature that resembled a dinosaur. Wash swore it was a spirit guardian of the sacred gold, and it so frightened him that he packed his camp and hastily departed."

Wash reportedly kept the bar of gold for many years as proof of his story. The rest of the gold horde still sits somewhere high in the mountains, guarded by a strange creature.

Water Babies

One especially creepy water monster legend that can be found in a number of states has its roots in Native American legends. Many tribes have distinct names for the creatures, but in English, they are commonly known as "water babies."

The creatures have some things in common with traditional mermaid tales, but they aren't limited to the ocean. Water babies can be found in lakes and rivers in the United States.

The creatures can take various forms, most of which are used to lure humans to their deaths. They can appear as a beautiful woman to seduce lone hunters, or they can take the form of a baby to appear vulnerable and in need of help.

Often, humans are simply taken to their deaths in the depths of the water; in other tales, water babies devour human flesh.

Around many bodies of water, people report hearing the weird cries of the water babies calling out in the night. By many accounts, hearing their cries is an ill omen.

In Utah, the White River and Provo River both reportedly once had water babies living in them.

Utah Lake is said to have been home to the creatures in the past and Green Lake, on the west side of the mountain southeast of Cedar City, was known to the natives as "Paingup'ee Kawneev" (Water Babies House).

In an April 29, 2006, article for the *Daily Herald*, Dr. Robert Carter notes that when Mormon pioneers arrived in the Great Basin, they heard stories of the water babies from the Ute people.

Carter reports that the LDS *Journal History* contains what may be the earliest pioneer reference related to the creatures.

It comes from the Southern Exploring Expedition that traveled south through the Utah Valley in November 1849. The party, led by Parley P. Pratt, made camp on November 29 at Punjun Spring, a body now known as Burraston Ponds. The entry reports:

"That evening the men gathered for a camp meeting. They sang hymns and two men who were ill received blessings. Toward the end of the meeting, Indian interpreter Dimick B. Huntington told the group about Ute Indian traditions, one of which was that the spring near which they camped was bottomless.

"The *Journal History* listing for this date tells of another Ute belief that Huntington may have told the men: 'The Indians have a tradition that this spring is inhabited by a hairy being, like a child 8 years old...he comes up at nights, make a noise like a frog and tries to frighten and catch Indians and draw them into this bottomless spring.'"

In *Ute Tales*, Anne M. Smith notes that a native woman referred to as "Old Mary," tells of water babies being heard around Ouray Lake.

Smith collected a number of water baby stories from members of the Ute Nation for her book. One account, from an elder named Archup, tells of a man hearing what sounded like a baby crying. The man went to the river (location not given) and saw a water baby "sitting on the water." The man threw a stick at the creature and the water baby went away.

The man may have run the creature off, but he paid a price— he started having dreams of rising water that was coming to get him. The man also became ill.

Stories like this one give us an indication of the close connection between the physical and spiritual worldview of the Ute people and a glimpse of just how blurry the lines between them are at times.

Concerning the water babies, Archup noted that "water babies are about the size of a man's hand. They have long, black hair. They cry just like babies."

John Duncan told Smith that the creatures once lived in the water somewhere near Vernal. Duncan said the things "cried like babies" and were "about the size of a three-year-old child."

Duncan also reported that there was a water baby around Provo. The elder tells the story of a boy named John who went with a friend to get a look at the creatures:

"John went fishing with this boy. They saw a Water Baby nearby, which was crying. The boy wanted to go back and look at it, but John was frightened and did not want to go. The Water Babies were on a flat rock. They had long hair.

"When the boys came near they dived into the water. The hair floated on top. When the Water Babies went under the water, the water started to rise and the boys ran away."

Fish Lake in Sevier County is also reportedly the home of water babies. There are several legends that surround the lake, some of a ghostly nature. Legend says a young Native American man died by the lake under mysterious circumstances. Some said he was murdered, while other tales claimed he had been killed by a water monster that came from the lake.

In *Lost Landscapes*, Utah author Linda Dunning notes that the man's spirit still haunts the lakeshore, continuing, in his afterlife, to hunt and fish the area he loved so much.

Dunning says the lake's monster legend varies, but one version involves "small serpent-like creatures that snatched people from the banks or pulled them under while they were swimming in the lake."

Curiously, while there are no recent accounts of water babies at Fish Lake, there have been reports of Bigfoot sightings in the area.

The mermaid-like version of water babies turns up plenty of times in Utah tales, too. Smith's book *Ute Tales* mentions the following account from Archup:

"Sometimes a young man would go to water the horses in the morning. If the water baby is female, the young man goes to sleep on the bank. When he wakes he feels someone lying beside him. He looks and see a beautiful woman in a green

117

dress lying there. He sleeps with her. After a while she coaxes him to go with her under the water. His family will never see him again because he goes under the water to her people."

Another Ute elder, Pearl Perika, told Smith that she knew a story about a man who was pulled into a river by a pair of female water babies. She also reports that there were many places where it was dangerous to even go near the water:

"When you tried to get water, the hands of the water people would try to pull you under the water. A man was afraid to draw water. The water baby women cry like babies."

Perika told another grimmer tale that highlights the monstrous hunger of the creatures.

According to the account, a group of people were camped by a river and a woman left her baby in a cradleboard leaning against a tree while she went to gather berries with the other women.

The child woke up and started to cry. A water baby heard the sound, came out of the river, and devoured the child. The creature then crawled into the cradleboard and took the form of the child it had eaten.

The now disguised water baby started crying and the mother returned. She picked up what she thought was her child and started nursing it.

She quickly realized that something was wrong and called for help. The other women who were picking berries rushed to her side and discovered that the water baby had devoured the woman's breast and was still going. As Perika reports:

"They tried to cut off the breast but could not do it. Water baby kept on swallowing until it swallowed the mother.

"The women told the husband what had happened to his wife and his baby. At the same place, later on, he heard a woman crying and said, 'That is my wife crying.' He went to get his wife. He went to the river and was pulled into the water by the Water Babies."

BEEHIVE STATE MONSTERS by David Weatherly

Panguitch Lake

Panguitch Lake, located in the Dixie National Forest in southwestern Garfield County, is said to house a giant... something. The lake's name itself comes from a Paiute word that means "big fish."

The lake is known for its trout, but when settlers arrived in the region in 1873, they heard stories from native people that the lake was home to a family of monsters. Local lore still mentions a "family of monsters" once living in the lake, though there's no real body of historic accounts on record, nor have there been any modern sightings of note.

The most significant piece of the puzzle regarding this tale appears to be an article that ran in the September 21, 1878, edition of the *Salt Lake Herald* under the headline "A Lake Legend: The Monster of Panguitch Lake: What the Indians Say of Him, His Coming and His Going."

The article includes a lengthy tale purportedly told by local native tribes about a monster that killed a hundred native women. The creature's murderous streak continued until one warrior led a band of men to storm the lake and confront the beast.

The account is likely not even rooted in native lore, but rather a typical fabricated "news" account of the day.

BEEHIVE STATE MONSTERS by David Weatherly

Moon Lake

Moon Lake is in the southern end of the Uintas at an elevation of 8,300 feet. The lake's name is derived from its shape—that of a crescent moon.

Moon Lake sits deep in the Ashley National Forest about thirty miles from Duchesne. The lake is not very well known and there are several folkloric traditions associated with it. Purportedly, the lake is home to a monster, though some believe this is an old folktale created years ago to deter those seeking gold in the region.

Some who visit the lake find it a bit eerie, and there are some unusual features to be found. According to officials with the Ashley National Forest, studies have found that parts of the lake have no discernible bottom. This has led some to believe that there are underground passages deep in the lake that connect it to other areas of the state.

I spoke to one Utah resident who told me there were several stories of people seeing a large, serpent-like creature in the lake, though he could not provide me with any direct witnesses to interview.

In *Haunted Utah*, author Andy Weeks reports that an entry in his grandmother Dora Mae Week's self-published life history discusses the monster.

"He [Gary Sutherland] said [in 1994] that the lake would be calm, even mirror-glassy with no wind or boats to create a wake."

Such conditions could only be found at the lake in the early morning or at dusk. Through the rest of the day, wind would create ripples on the lake's surface. Week's book reports:

"One would see a V-shaped ripple moving slowly but

steadily through the center of the lake, usually coming from the north end, and zigzagging but mostly running closer to the far shore. He said it would appear like a rounded object pushing water in front of itself, moving smoothly enough to create a ripple but not a breaking wave."

Drinking coffee at daybreak one morning in the Moon Lake Lodge, the witness saw something unusual in the water, grabbed binoculars, and went outside to get a clear look at the object:

"I focused the binoculars again on the apex of the V as it approached the near shore. The binoculars gave me clear enough sight to know this was no beaver.

"I observed the apex from the back and could see nothing breaking the surface, only the rounded push of water at one point, seeming just below the surface. The point looked the same, coming and going."

The object was the only thing moving on the lake. It zigzagged toward the far shore and traveled near the witness. The creature headed away but nothing more of it ever came into clear view. Weeks's book further states:

"It's common knowledge in the area that such a creature might really exist. I heard the stories myself when I was a child, and once while fishing with my family from the lake's sandy shore, I imagined a Loch Ness Monster-type creature raising its serpent head from the water and staring at me."

It's interesting to note that there have been Bigfoot sightings around Moon Lake. Perhaps the monsters are drawn together!

Moon Lake

BEEHIVE STATE MONSTERS by David Weatherly

Sevier Lake

A Paiute story from Sevier Lake involves a monster fish capable of swallowing men whole. LaVan Martineau recounts the tale in *Southern Paiutes Legend, Lore, Language and Lineage*.

According to the story, two men were chasing antelope near the lake when they spotted a whirlpool in the water. One of the men swam out to see what was causing the disruption while the other watched from shore.

The man swimming in the lake was suddenly swallowed whole by a giant fish. The man's friend, knife in hand, swam out to save his companion. He, too, was swallowed whole by the giant fish, but it wasn't the end of the story. According to LaVan:

"After the fish swallowed him, he ended up lying right alongside his friend inside the fish's belly. He then felt around for a soft spot in the belly, and when he found it, he cut the belly open, and they got out. As they got out, the fish didn't move, but afterward as it was dying, it wiggled violently and splashed water all over and those two guys almost didn't get away. The bones of this fish could be seen in this lake for a long time."

LaVan notes that he originally heard the tale from Carl Jake of Indian Peake, but that he later heard the same account from another person who placed the event at Utah Lake.

The tale is interesting and perhaps indicates that fossilized bones of some prehistoric giant were once easily seen at the lake.

Sevier Lake is in Millard County and is semi-dry. In the mid-1800s, settlers in the region started diverting water from the Sevier River for irrigation, which depleted water from the lake. By 1878 Sevier Lake was almost completely dry and since that time it has been intermittent.

It's fed primarily by the Beaver and Sevier Rivers and is a remnant of the Pleistocene Lake Bonneville.

Being mostly dry and with low levels of water, it's unlikely that the lake was the home of anything monstrous in modern history and at least some of the stories were likely a reflection of the monster craze created by the stories coming from Bear Lake about its monster.

Sevier Lake

Lake Powell

Lake Powell is a man-made lake on the Utah/Arizona border. It stretches across three Utah counties: Garfield, Kane, and San Juan on the Utah side. The lake was created by the flooding of Glen Canyon when the Glen Canyon Dam was constructed.

Lake Powell is the second largest artificial reservoir in the United States, right behind Nevada's Lake Mead. Lake Powell is also a popular vacation destination and receives an estimated two million visitors each year.

A sixty-two-year-old aerospace financial planner named J. Greenwald spotted something very unusual in Lake Powell—a giant beaver, one that was the size of a horse!

Greenwald reported her sighting to the National Institute of Discovery Science (NIDS) in Las Vegas. Although she filed the report in 2002, she said that the sighting had taken place two years before—in 2000.

Greenwald and some friends were out on a boat in the lake. She recalls that conditions that day were clear, and it was around 5 p.m. The creature remained in view for approximately fifteen minutes. Greenwald reports:

"You wouldn't believe how big it was. It could kill you. Lake Powell is hundreds of miles of unknown unsearched water where such a creature could easily hide and obviously has for a long time. I would not post this here, but I don't know where else to tell this story. We couldn't believe it when we saw it. It was not a normal beaver."

The creature was between 50 and 100 feet away from the boat and was near Bullfrog Marina. The animal was brown to black in color and weighed in the range of 700-900 pounds.

Loren Coleman spoke with Greenwald about her sighting. She told him that the creature was the size of a medium sized horse or a large bear. She told Coleman:

"It had huge front teeth and large back legs and was not, in our opinion, a normal beaver. It definitely had beaver-like characteristics, but it was more of a prehistoric type animal that was so large that we were all in shock."

In *The Field Guide to Lake Monsters, Sea Serpents, and other Mystery Denizens of the Deep*, by Loren Coleman and Patrick Huyghe, Coleman points to the possibility of a surviving giant beaver--*Castoroides ohioensis*—a creature that was the size of a black bear, measured almost 8 feet in length, and weighed 600 to 700 pounds. It had massive convex incisor teeth measuring six inches in length.

Some fossil evidence of the creature has been discovered and evidence indicates the animal had wide ranging distribution. According to Coleman:

"Some of the more complete fossils come from Ohio where the giant beaver lived concurrently with humans less than 10,000 years ago. A possible Castoroides ohioensis lodge was discovered near New Knoxville, Ohio, in 1912."

The wilds of Utah would certainly be an ideal place for a surviving giant beaver to dwell, and it's one of the theories that may explain some anomalous water creature sightings in the state.

Lake Powell

BEEHIVE STATE MONSTERS by David Weatherly

Bottle Hollow

Bottle Hollow is a strange place. First and foremost, it's right next door to Skinwalker Ranch. That alone, perhaps, puts more attention on the curious things reported at the site.

Bottle Hollow is a man-made reservoir on Ute tribal land. It's 420 acres and was filled with fresh water in 1970.

The site's name comes from the wild west days when the ravine was empty of water. The spot became a popular dumping ground for empty whiskey bottles. In fact, the ravine became so full of them that it became known as Bottle Hollow, a name that stuck into modern times.

The reservoir today is a popular spot for fishing and there are a lot of strange mysteries connected to it, including reports of strange lights coming out of, and sometimes going into, the water. People have also reported UFOs around Bottle Hollow, and like the lights, the UFOs sometimes dive into the water or fly out of it.

According to the Utes, the water at Bottle Hollow is inhabited by one, or several, large aquatic snakes. These creatures resemble the classic sea serpents of myth and legend and are purportedly dangerous. Sightings of the creatures at Bottle Hollow reportedly go back to the time when the ravine was first filled with water, though most of the accounts seem to be oral tales told and retold through the years.

Colm and Kelleher mention Bottle Hollow in their book *Hunt for the Skinwalker*. They report hearing the following from a tribal police officer:

"'We used to see things crawling around in the water that looked like giant snakes,' he told us. '[It] would swim straight down from the marina and go all the way down to the bottom end. You could see it on moonlit nights. I have seen that, well, everybody, the other guys have seen that snake in there, too.'"

Hunt for the Skinwalker also notes the following:

"Tribal police officers say an inordinate number of drowning cases have occurred in Bottle Hollow over the years, and at least some of them are unofficially attributed to the presence of the mystery snake."

A Ute woman swimming in the water one night was suddenly attacked by something beneath the surface. She called out, screaming for help as she was being pulled under.

Her male companion dove under the water to save her and confronted the attacker—a giant snake. The man struggled to free the woman and finally did so, but it was too late, she had drowned during the struggle.

Witnesses on the beach at the time confirmed the events from their perspective, confirming the woman's calls for help and her reports that something beneath the water had grabbed her.

Bottle Hollow

BEEHIVE STATE MONSTERS by David Weatherly

Invasive Species

In the summer of 2006 Scott Clements and his son Jack were fishing on Utah Lake near the Provo boat harbor. Feeling a pull on the line, the men reeled in what they first thought was a thirteen-inch bluegill, but a closer look at the fish gave them a surprise.

"That's a piranha, Dad!" Jack declared when he got a look at the vicious row of incisors in the fish's mouth.

The Clementses contacted the state's Department of Wildlife Resources (DWR) who took the fish into their possession. They later identified it as a pacu—a South American freshwater fish related to the more well-known piranha. Pacu have teeth similar to their relatives, though they are traditionally vegetarian. In their native home, pacu survive primarily by eating fruit that falls into the water from overhanging trees.

The general consensus was that the fish had been someone's exotic pet. KSL News spoke with DWR official Scott Root about the fish. Root told the news:

"The main difference is a piranha has an underbite whereas the pacu has almost more of an overbite.

"This is the second time I've heard of (pacu) in Utah Lake. What happens is people don't know what to do with them. They can't kill them—they don't have the heart. So, they do something even worse and put them in some water somewhere."

Pacu can reach up to thirty inches when fully grown, so the specimen pulled up by Clements was still growing.

News of the exotic fish created a stir in the community and for a time, people were concerned that the lake was infested with flesh-eating fish, but Root emphasized that although the fish weren't native to the area, they weren't as dangerous as people feared.

"They don't bother you unless you're cut or bleeding or something like that. The natives in South America swim with them," Root said.

It was doubtful that more pacu were in the lake and most likely the one caught by the Clements was a specimen dumped from someone's home aquarium.

The concern about piranha wasn't necessarily unfounded since the creatures have been discovered in Utah waters in the past. In the summer of 1985 wildlife officials were alerted about the discovery of piranha in a small pond on the west side of Ogden.

Steve Norgia and his friend Terry Miller were fishing on the pond one day when they pulled up what they first thought was a carp. When Miller tried to pick the fish up by its gills, it nipped at his fingers and the men spotted the creature's teeth. They placed the fish in a bathtub and contacted wildlife officials.

Wildlife enforcement specialist Bruce Johnson looked at the fifteen-inch specimen and said that it was the first time piranha had been found in the wild in the state.

The size of the fish concerned officials who decided to net the Ogden River in case there were more of the little flesh eaters. There are no natural predators for piranha in Utah, so officials worried that if the fish survived the winter, they could start thriving in the state.

In 2002, several piranhas were caught in the Jordan River, and the same year, several were found in Decker Lake.

Exotic fish that have been released into the wild have been a serious problem in Utah over the years, and wildlife officials have made an effort to crack down on the trade of illegal exotic animals in the state. Invasive species can decimate native fish populations and moving fish from one body of water to another Utah is a class A misdemeanor.

Mark Magnera of St. George pulled in a nine-pound pacu on June 12, 2015. Magnera caught the fish in a warm water pond known to locals as "The Boiler." The pond had been closed by city officials for fifteen years and only recently reopened to the public when Magnera snagged the fish. Magnera told reporters with the *KSL News*:

"We go down there and the first thing I see is two, big dark fish. And I'm a fisherman so I wanted to catch one of them. So, I came back the next day and I caught one and I had no idea what it was."

After catching the fish, Magnera took photos of it, then released it back into the water, thinking that it was possibly an endangered species. He showed the photographs to wildlife officials who confirmed that the fish was a pacu.

Richard Hepworth, DWR's southern region aquatics manager, said the Boiler had long been a dumping area for exotic fish:

"I remember when I was a kid 35 years ago going down there and catching some really weird fish that had been dumped out of somebody's aquarium. People get these aquarium fish. They like them for a long time, but then one day, they get sick of having to clear the aquarium or something and people have a hard time killing their pets."

Hepworth says that the Boiler is fed by a warm water spring which keeps the water at a consistent 72-75 degrees. Under such conditions, exotic fish can survive and thrive.

Magnera told *KSL News* reporters that he had seen hundreds of the fish swimming in the Boiler and that the fish was challenging to catch. "It's the weirdest, biggest fish I've caught. I've caught like 12-pound catfish out of Utah Lake and none of them put up the fight that those pacu did."

The Bear Lake Monster

Bear Lake is a natural freshwater lake straddling the borders of Utah and Idaho. The lake is 109 square miles and is divided evenly between the two states. It's a picturesque spot, sitting at an elevation of 5,924 feet. It's known for its turquoise blue water, a feature that helped the lake earn its nickname, "Caribbean of the Rockies."

The lake is over 250,000 years old, and its water properties have led to the evolution of several unique species of fauna. With a maximum depth of about 208 feet, the lake is a popular spot for outdoor enthusiasts who enjoy boating, camping, hiking and other activities around the water.

The lake is also home to a legendary creature—the Bear Lake monster.

As with many monsters from the pioneer days, descriptions of the creature vary widely. By some accounts, the beast is a hundred feet in length and resembles a serpent. Its body is light cream in color, and it moves through the water faster than a locomotive. The creature's head resembles that of a cow, or perhaps a walrus, and it has a voracious appetite.

Other stories say the creature is a mere fifty feet in length and resembles a snake with feet and the head of a crocodile or alligator.

Even today, if you ask locals around Bear Lake to describe the monster, you'll receive a range of answers from vague, Loch Ness monster-like descriptions to a simple "it's a giant fish" response.

Others of course will offer a quiet chuckle and a shake of the head at the absurdity of a possible monster in the lake. The question of the monster is, at the least, controversial since one of its early proponents admitted to fabricating the tale. But let's take it from the beginning.

Native Americans in the region told stories about strange things associated with Bear Lake for many years before the pioneer tales began. Explorer John C. Fremont was at Bear Lake in 1843 and heard accounts from Shoshone and Bannock lore that described a race of monsters that reportedly lived in the water.

According to an article by A. J. Simmonds in *True Frontier* magazine (January 1969 Vol 1 No 7):

"Legend had it that a young brave had fallen in love with a woman of an enemy tribe. Both sides were angry and set guards to watch the pair. They were discovered at a secret rendezvous by both tribes, who pursued them along the shores of Bear Lake. Just as they were to be overtaken, the Great Spirit changed them into enormous fish and sent them into the lake where, periodically, they and their descendants revenged themselves on the two tribes by devouring unsuspecting victims who happened to venture into the water."

The Shoshone dated the departure of the monsters to the bitter winter of 1830, the same winter that had killed the last of the buffalo in the Bear Lake Valley.

As more people began to settle in the region, they heard stories of monsters in the lake. Some thought the natives had made the tales up to try to keep people off the land. There were no recorded sightings until a man named Joseph Rich caught the public's attention with an article about the monster in 1868.

Rich's tales appeared in the *Deseret News* and the paper's August 3, 1868, edition started the ball rolling with a letter from Rich detailing the legends of the lake's creature.

According to the report, natives in the region had a long-standing tradition concerning a serpent-like creature that lived in the lake. Reportedly, the beast had been responsible for the deaths of many men through the years, although, Rich was told, the beast had not been seen "since the buffalo had inhabited the Valley." Still, the natives refused to swim in the lake or use it for bathing. For that matter, they wouldn't even sleep too close to it for fear the monster would emerge and take them.

Reportedly, the natives told Rich that the creature was serpent-like but had legs about eighteen inches long. The appendages allowed the beast to go ashore. It was also said to spurt water upwards out of its mouth.

Rich sounded the alarm because, according to him, the lake's "water devil" had suddenly resurfaced and was witnessed by settlers in the area. He writes:

"The Bear Lake Monster, they now call it, is causing a great deal of excitement up here. S.M. Johnson at South Eden was riding along near the Lake the other day when he saw something a number of yards out in the lake which he thought was the body of a man. He waited for the waves to wash it in, but to his surprise, found the water washed over it without causing it to move. Then he saw it had a head and neck like some strange animal. On each side of the head were ears or bunches the size of a pint cup. He concluded the body must be touching the bottom of the lake. By this time, however, Johnson seems to have been leaving the place so rapidly he failed to observe other details."

The paper reported that four more people saw the creature the day after the Johnson sighting. According to the witnesses, the creature was moving "faster than a horse could run."

Rich's article continued with an account from yet another group who reportedly saw the beast:

"On Sunday last, N.C. Davis and Allen Davis of St. Charles, Thomas Sleight and James Collings of Paris, with six women were returning from Fish Haven when about midway from the latter place to St. Charles, their attention was suddenly attracted to a peculiar motion of waves on the water about three miles distant. The lake was not rough, only a little disturbed by the wind. Mr. Sleight says he distinctly saw the sides of a very large animal that he would suppose to be not less than 90 feet in length."

One of the Davis men thought the creature was considerably smaller, estimating it in the forty-foot range. The group watched as the creature's movements created waves on the water. The beast was heading south, and the witnesses all agreed that it moved with incredible speed. The article continues:

"Mr. Davis says he never saw a locomotive travel faster, and thinks it made a mile a minute. In a few minutes after the discovery of the first, a second followed in its wake, but seemed much smaller, appearing to Mr. Sleight about the size of a horse. A larger one followed this, and so on until, before disappearing, it made a sudden turn to the west a short distance, then back to its former track. At this turn Mr. Sleight says he could distinctly see it was of a brown color. They could judge somewhat of the speed by observing known distances on the opposite side of the lake; and all agree that the velocity with which these monsters propelled themselves, was astounding. They represent the waves rolling up on each side as about three feet high."

Rich went on to emphasize the prominence and veracity of the witnesses, a common theme in early newspapers.

Once attention was put on the monster, the stories flowed, and other publications chimed in.

The Latter-Day Saints' Millennial Star Vol 30, 1868, reported on the following regarding the monster:

"We have had conversation with brother Charles C. Rich and other brethren from Bear Lake Valley, respecting the monsters which have been seen in the Lake, an account of which, from the pen of brother Joseph C. Rich, was published in the *Evening News* a short time ago. They all firmly believe the account as published. They consider the testimony that has been given by so many individuals, who have seen these creatures in so many places and under a variety of circumstances, indisputable. They would believe these persons upon any other subject, and they cannot withhold their credence—incredible as the existence of such monsters may appear—from what they say they saw in the Lake.

"We should conclude that there are very few, if any, persons in Bear Lake Valley who doubt the statements which have been made. The Indians' traditions corroborate all that has been said of these creatures. It is well known that the Indians will not camp near the Lake, and they have never been known to bathe in its waters. They have persisted in stating that there were terrible monsters in the Lake, of which they were in fear, two of their tribe having within the memory of some of their number, been carried off by them. If one or two persons only had seen and described them, it might be set down, even if they were persons of good judgement and credibility, as an optical delusion; but they have been lately seen by numbers, and at different times and places, and their descriptions agree, and they also agree with the accounts of the Indians. Various plans have been suggested for the capture of one or more of them, but no attempt has as yet been made. We hope that some plan may be devised that will be successful. Until the question of their existence is settled, and something learned of their nature and habits, if such monsters are actually there, the Lake will not be a very common place of resort for fishermen. One of these who are said to have seen them last, timed their speed while passing from one well known point to another on the other side of the Lake, with his watch, and if the description can be relied upon, a boat would stand no chance of escaping if they were pursued or came in contact with it. Our readers who are familiar with the accounts we have published of these creatures, can form their own conclusions respecting them. The accounts are fishy, decidedly so; but we cannot Dispute the persons who make them. Some of the persons who have seen them we know, and their truthfulness is unquestionable. We must believe they saw something remarkable, whether monsters or not we hope time will soon decide."

The August 5, 1868, edition of the *Deseret News* reported: "Monsters of Bear Lake," and Rich attempted to claim that sightings of the Bear Lake monster predated sightings of Nessie, the monster reputed to live in Loch Ness in Scotland.

"All lakes, caves and dens have their legendary histories. Tradition loves to throw her magic wand over beautiful dells and lakes, and people them with fairies, giants, and monsters of various kinds. Bear Lake has also its own monster tale to tell, and when I have told it, I will leave you to judge whether or not its merits are merely traditionary."

*Mormon President Brigham Young was interested
in the Bear Lake Monster accounts*

In 1869 a party led by President Brigham Young visited the Bear Lake Valley. Young was purportedly on the lookout for the lake monster but didn't have any personal experiences. He did, however, write that he had spoken to people in the area who had seen the beast. Russell R. Rich notes in *Land of the Sky-Blue Water*:

"A family with whom Brother Woodruff and myself (Brigham Young) conversed…several members of which were in the company which saw the ten that were described in the *News Examiner* last summer speak so confidently and calmly upon the subject and describe so accurately the appearance of these creatures in the lake, that however much one may be disposed to be skeptical, he cannot but accord sincerity to them."

President Brigham Young was so interested in the creature that he made an arrangement with Phineas Cook of Swan Creek to catch the monster. Cook had spotted the creature himself one day and estimated that it moved a mile a minute.

Cook planned on using a large, barbed hook attached to twenty feet of cable, which in turn would be fastened to three hundred yards of one-inch-thick rope. The rope would be tied off to a large buoy with a large American flag on a staff and a sinker attached. The buoy, in turn, would be connected to a hundred yards of inch thick rope which would be tied off to a tree at the lakeshore.

Cook assumed that if the creature somehow broke one of the ropes, its location could still be determined by the buoy.

Cook spent the season trying to capture the beast but had no luck. He did report that the hook was stripped of the bait on several occasions, and he believed it was the monster that had made off with the meat.

The June 1, 1870, edition of the *Deseret News* ran a report from Charles C. Rich who said the lake monster had been spotted yet again. This time, a young man named Marion Thomas and three sons of Phineas H. Cook were out fishing in a boat. The group was near Swan Creek just north of Garden City, when Thomas spotted a creature with a serpent shaped head.

He saw about twenty feet of the thing's body which he said was covered with hair or fur. Two flippers extended from the upper part of the monster's body. The man said he was close enough to have shot the creature if he'd had a rifle.

The August 20, 1870, edition of the *Salt Lake Herald* told its readers that the lake monsters had become more active and reported that more citizens were starting to believe in the beast:

"Bishop Budge informs us the Bear Lake monster has been seen very frequently of late. Even the most skeptical are giving way. One reliable gentleman saw three of them together recently."

The next notable sighting was in 1870 and involved a pair of skeptics. According to the account in Thompson's *Folklore in the Bear Lake Valley*:

"Two skeptics, Thomas Rich and Milando Pratt, were traveling along the borders of the lake when the conversation turned to the monster; each expressed the idea that the sight of one would gratify him. A short while later there was much commotion in the lake and they saw part of the body of a creature that was larger around than the body of a man, the head resembling a walrus minus the tusks. 'The portion of the body out of the water was ten feet long.' The entire length of the creature was about forty feet. It swam toward the east side of the lake with the motion of a serpent, and the two men viewed it for about fifteen minutes."

Thompson also notes the large number of accounts from people who reportedly spotted the creature at the lake.

"Among them were Elizabeth W.H. Johnson of Randolph, Utah, and her cousin, Lottie Pead. They claimed that one day as they were wading in the lake, they saw a monster flop out of the water on the far side of the lake. The water splashed high in the air several times. They were frightened and hurried to the bank, gathered up their clothes, and ran up the hill to their homes which were close by."

The tales continued throughout the 1870s. In The *Field Guide to Lake Monsters, Sea Serpents, and Other Mystery Denizens of the Deep*, authors Loren Coleman and Patrick Huyghe mention a sighting reported by another Mormon pioneer.

On Friday, May 15, 1874, three men on their way home were passing by Bear Lake when they spotted an object in the water, about twenty yards from shore.

One of the men, William Budge, was a well-known wagon train captain. He stated:

"At first sight we thought it might be a very large duck." As the men got closer, they realized it was something more unusual.

"Its face and part of its head were distinctly seen, covered with fur, or short hair of a light snuff color."

Budge said the creature had very large full eyes spaced wide like a cow's. The face, he said, resembled that of a fox and the ears were prominent. The man estimated that the creature's neck was four or five feet long.

He reported that the creature did not seem ferocious and did not appear to be in any hurry, moving slowly while the men observed it. Finally, it dove, came back up, and moved off into the lake at about the same speed as a man walking.

The same year (1874) noted traveler John Codman came through the Bear Lake Valley. According to *Land of the Sky-Blue Water*, by Dr. Russell R. Rich, Codman had this to say about the creature:

"There is really good reason to believe that the lake is inhabited by some abnormal water animals. We conversed with seven persons, among them our friend, Bishop Rich, who at different times had seen them; and they told us that many other individuals could verify their report. The length of the monsters varies from thirty to eighty feet, and their bodies are covered with fur like that of a seal. The head is described like that of an alligator. In one instance the animal came close to shore and was entangled in the rushes, where he squirmed and splashed, and made a horrible noise like the roaring of a bull."

In 1881 another attempt to capture the creature was launched. According to the August 27, 1881, edition of the *Ogden Herald*, a group of fishermen had set out to snare the elusive beast. The paper noted that it couldn't account for the "absolute correctness" of the story, but it went on to tell the tale under the headline "A Sucker for Sheep." According to the *Herald*, a team of would-be monster hunters had slaughtered a sheep to use as bait in their attempts to snag the massive creature in the water. The carcass was used to bait a grappling hook which was attached to a long rope and lowered into the lake. The rope was tied off and the men left the scene, confident that they would return to find the creature helplessly hooked.

According to the news, a group of natives had quietly watched the procedure and were disgusted by the waste of perfectly good mutton. Once the fishermen left the scene, the natives promptly pulled the line out of the water and retrieved the sheep carcass. They replaced the sheep with what the paper calls "the largest of the sucker species they could find."

No doubt the fishermen were puzzled by the switch when they returned and the paper noted that "instead of the mysterious product of the placid Northern Lake, the enterprising anglers succeeded in getting a sucker."

In 1894 Joseph C. Rich wrote a long letter to the *Bear Lake Democrat* (republished in the April 17, 1947, edition of the *News Examiner* of Montpelier, Idaho). In the letter, Rich detailed aspects of his life and career in the valley and stated:

"I discovered and made famous by publication in the *Deseret News* that wonderful first class lie—'The Bear Lake Monster.'"

While the statement seems to be both an admission of guilt and an indication that the entire monster tale is fabricated, not everyone was convinced. After all, there were many other accounts through the years so either numerous people were in on the hoax, or they were mistaken in their observations.

Rich's admission didn't completely deter reports of the monster, though it certainly did add a different spin to the tales which continued to morph into a curious blend of folklore, storytelling, parody and even politics.

On September 18, 1907, the *Logan Republican* ran a headline about the creature: "Bear Lake Monster Appears. Leviathan

Comes from Lake and Devours Horse While Men Shoot At It." The story offered yet another description of the strange creature:

"The Bear Lake Monster, a combination of dragon, bear and fish, and measuring twenty feet in length and possessing the roar of a lion, is again agitating the people over the mountains."

The paper wrote a follow up a few days later and the story became even more bizarre. The headline in the September 21, 1907, edition announced:

"Quil Nebeker Sees Monster"

The subject of the story, Quil Nebeker, was Aquilla C. Nebeker, a well-known public figure who had served as President of the Senate of Utah and had once been acting governor of the state.

One would expect that such an upstanding citizen would provide solid facts regarding the potential lake monster. Instead, Nebeker wrote a long, and very odd, account of his encounter with the creature. Nebeker claimed that the beast came up out of the water and devoured eight of his sheep. Apparently, this wasn't enough for the beast, and it continued to rage across Nebeker's farm eating eight of the man's pigs, a stack of hay and a dozen bales of barbed wire. Nebeker clearly needed to calm the creature down and he quickly found the solution. He writes:

"I noticed my large graphophone standing on the table ready for use. An inspiration struck me—I called to mind the value of music in taming the snakes and wild animals of the forest and I decided to try it."

Nebeker goes on to recount his meeting with the monster and the tune they played together, ending the tale with a statement on the so-called monster:

"Now, boys, this is the straight of that 'Bear Lake Monster' story, but don't call him a 'monster' any longer, for he is truly wondrously human."

Of course, Nebeker's "wondrous" account, written in the style of the day, doesn't provided us with...well, much of anything other than a weird anecdote to the entire Bear Lake

Monster lore.

It's unclear what kind of point the politician was making. Perhaps he just wanted to have some fun. Whatever the case, rumors spread about a politician seeing the monster and pieces of the account have shown up frequently when people look at the monster tale.

A young boy named Ronald W. Hansen had a very close encounter with the monster in 1937. The tale was verified years later—1974 to be exact—by Idaho reporter Bonnie Thompson of the *Lava News*. The tale was later examined by writer Will Bagley for the October 5, 2003, edition of the *Salt Lake Tribune*.

The four-year-old Hansen was playing on a 12-foot plank on Bear Lake when the wind blew him out into the water. The boy ended up more than a mile offshore and was in water 90 foot deep. The *Tribune* reports:

"Ronald struggled to stay afloat until a long, serpentine head emerged from the water and two reptilian eyes sized him up as a possible snack. 'I saw him,' Ronald said later. The lad did what any resourceful Utah youth would do: 'I hit him with a little stick!'"

Ronald was pulled up by a rescuer in a boat just before he went under water for good.

Utah folklorist Austin E. Fife states that a boy named Preston Pond, a Cache Valley Boy Scout, spotted the monster in 1946. Unfortunately, I have not located any details of the sighting.

In her book *Folklore in the Bear Lake Valley*, Bonnie Thompson recounts an interesting sighting from the 1960s. The author interviewed Glade Myler of Cove, Utah, who said the incident occurred in the spring of 1961:

"A troop of scouts chaperoned by my father and a friend were at Camp Hunt located near Lakota. I went out in a rowboat with the rest of the scouts, and father and his companion stayed at the camp. They were standing on the shore watching the lake, when a huge body arose from the water, making huge waves as it rose. It appeared for only a few minutes, traveling south, then slowly sank and disappeared as mysteriously as it had appeared. My father thoroughly believes to this day he saw the famous Bear Lake Monster."

Bear Lake—home of a monster?

Through the years, people have continued to look at the lake with a certain curiosity. Despite Rich's admission that he fabricated stories, many people still wonder if there's any truth to tales of monstrous creatures in the lake and, at the least, unusual things have been reported in the water.

The November 19, 1976, edition of Bountiful's *Davis County Clipper* ran a story about a curious incident involving a herd of elk at Bear Lake.

Bryce Nielson, a biologist with the state's Division of Wildlife Resources Fisheries, reported that on October 24, he watched a herd of seventeen elk take to the water. The herd was caught near the edge of the lake and found their path to the mountains blocked by the highway, so they took to the water and started swimming. Nielson watched as the lead animal herded the others, keeping them together as they made their

155

way toward South Eden Point.

Nielson was surprised at the sight and monitored the herd's movements. They swam almost seven miles, a task that took them three and a half hours to accomplish.

The elk settled in for the night at South Eden Point with a herd of cows. Nielson expected that the elk would head for higher ground in the night, but to his surprise, the next day, the herd was in the water and returned back seven miles to the point where they had entered for their first swim.

The biologist spoke with locals about the event, but they all stated that they had never seen such a performance. The unusual event provoked some thought of the lake's monster mystery. As the paper reports:

"Nielson mentioned that looking at the small herd of elk in the middle of the lake made him and other residents think about the legend of the Bear Lake Monster. Could it be that we have solved another mystery?"

Elk numbers in the area are small, so at the least, the sighting was an unusual one. Their presence in the water and the way they carefully navigated with a lead animal keeping them together, shows that it's probably not the first time the animals had to navigate a large body of water.

In *Lost Landscapes*, author Linda Dunning mentions a 1994 sighting at the lake. Reportedly, a general manager and four construction workers spotted something odd in the water. The group was working on the multi-million-dollar Harbor Village Hotel and Restaurant when they observed a "huge, agile object moving through the water."

No further details are on record, and some people dismissed the account as either another elk sighting or a publicity ploy by the business owners.

In 2000, Conrad Nebeker of Indian Creek constructed a 65-foot monster boat. Built to look like a giant green serpent, the vessel was christened the Bear Lake Monster Boat. Nebeker later sold the boat to Brian Hirschi who used it to ferry tourists around the lake.

Hirschi claimed he encountered the lake monster in June 2002. His incident occurred on a summer night while he was anchoring his boat. After tossing the anchor, he spotted a pair of humps in the water about a hundred yards from his boat. At first, he thought he was seeing some lost water skis floating in the water, but the objects vanished from sight. Moments later, his boat was lifted. Hirschi says:

"I started to get scared. The next thing I know, a serpent-like creature shot up out of the water; it had really dark, slimy green skin and deep beet-red eyes."

Hirschi says the creature went back underwater, then there was a loud sound "like a roaring bull." The creature took off through the water and was gone.

Concerned about what people would think, Hirschi didn't report the encounter right away, but after a time, he broke his silence and told his tale. "Once you've seen the monster," Hirschi said, "you really don't care what other people say."

Of course, many people did doubt Hirschi's story, pointing out that, with his business, the man had a vested interest in tourism at the lake.

An *Associated Press* story datelined July 11, 2004, takes a skeptical view of Hirschi's account. Reporter Mark Thiessen wrote:

"The only thing not in question is the monster's ability to make cash registers sing at stores ringing the lake on the Idaho-Utah border.

"The 168-year-old tale got new fins when Bear Lake business owner Brian Hirschi recently announced that he had seen the creature. But skeptics were quick to point out that his recounting of the 2-year-old sighting appeared in a Salt Lake newspaper on Memorial Day weekend—the start of the summer tourist season."

The Bear Lake Monster hit the news again in 2016 with a headline that declared "Remains of Mysterious Creature Discovered at Bear Lake."

The story quickly made the rounds on the Internet and a

photo of a strange carcass accompanied the article. The report caught the attention of many Utah residents as well as local news stations in Salt Lake City.

The carcass had reportedly been discovered by James and Christina Wilson who were walking along the lake shore. The couple reportedly said the carcass looked like a "rotting dinosaur."

Utah wildlife official Dr. Brian Upton was quoted as stating:

"It seems obvious that this creature was some kind of large marine predator, but the exact nature of the animal is yet to be determined. It definitely looks a lot like a crocodile but has a few distinct features which suggest that it could be another type of aquatic reptile. The creature's jaw seems very similar to various types of mosasaurs, some aquatic reptiles which used to live in many American lakes."

Logan's *Herald Journal* reported on the news of the purported monster carcass. According to the story in the February 16, 2016, edition of the paper:

"A story making the rounds on the Internet about a strange creature washed up on the shore of Bear Lake is a hoax, the Utah Division of Wildlife Resources said Tuesday."

The widely circulated photo and article about the carcass claimed that the body of a mysterious creature had been investigated by Utah Wildlife official Brian Upton who compared the creature to a mosasaur, a marine animal from the Cretaceous Period. But the *Herald* reported some problems with the account:

"The problem is, the Utah DWR has no official named Brian Upton and the Bear Lake couple quoted in the article also appears fabricated.

"DWR spokeswoman Amy Canning said she caught wind of the fantastic story through social media along with other Utahns on Tuesday, and she insisted with a chuckle there is absolutely no truth to it."

A reverse image search revealed that the carcass photo had been used previously in stories about other purported water monster discoveries.

So, what, if anything is in the lake? In her book *Between Pulpit and Pew*, folklorist Elaine Thatcher offers her opinion:

"My research in the Bear Lake Valley shows that the monster story has now evolved into self-parody, as locals play with the story, for themselves and for tourists."

The statement seems to sum up the general attitude surrounding Bear Lake. The monster has been part of the region's folklore for so long that many people often have no idea what's genuine and what's clever storytelling.

The creature, sometimes called Isabella, has been featured in various media including a 2009 episode of *Animal Planet's* cryptid themed show *The Lost Tapes*.

Whether it's a complete fabrication or the lingering legend of some long-lost creature, the Bear Lake Monster is a firm part of local lore in Northern Utah.

Utah Lake

Utah Lake lies in the middle of Utah County near the Provo-Orem metropolitan area in Utah Valley. It's a freshwater lake twenty-four miles in length and thirteen miles in width with a surface area of 95,000 acres. With a maximum depth of fourteen feet, it seems an unlikely place to find a monster, but one was purportedly spotted in 1864.

Henry Walker of Lehi was at the lake when he saw what looked like a giant snake with the head of a greyhound.

Shortly afterwards, Walker corresponded with the *Deseret News*, providing them with more news of the monster. The paper's September 2, 1868, edition contains the accounts sent to them by Walker. It reports:

"Some three or four years ago Bro. Isaac Fox was hunting along the lake, south of Lehi, and when about a mile and a half east of the head of Jordan, while creeping around a point of rushes in the water to get a shot at some geese, he heard a noise and, looking eastward, he saw what he supposed at the first glace was an animal, but he soon discovered it looked like a snake. He made for the shore, and it followed, until it came within about two rods of him. He said its head was like a greyhound's, and its eyes were deep black and piercing. It turned and swam across the lake and was soon followed by another of a darker color than the first. They seemed about twenty-five or thirty feet long, and swam straight in the water, faster than a man could run."

Walker also reported that a year after the Fox sighting, Canute Peterson's son saw a similar beast a quarter of a mile from the spot where Fox had seen the creatures he reported.

Shortly after that, he says, two men cutting hay along the

lakeside had an encounter. The men were about a half mile east of the Peterson sighting location. They had cut wild hay from one area and were searching for another spot to gather more when they saw something strange in the lake. As reported in the *News*:

"They had a dog with them, and hearing a splashing, they went down into the rushes, near the water, supposing it was the dog after something, when a creature raised itself up, some three rods off them, and looked them full in the face."

The two men fled in different directions, one climbing up a ridge. Once at a safe spot, he turned and looked at the creature. The *News* continues:

"He said its head was a foot across and shaped like a greyhound's; and it had the wickedest-looking black eyes he had ever seen. It darted its tongue out which was red and forked. The color of the 'snake' was a deep yellow with black spots."

In 1870, tales of monsters in the area were further fueled by the discovery of an unusual skull. The September 14, 1870, edition of the *Deseret News*, reported on the skull find with a note from Springville dated the previous week (September 7). The report stated:

"The Messrs. Dallin of this place, well known for their fishing proclivities, while plying their favorite vocation on the shores of the lake, found a section of skull of the Lake Monster, at least all who have examined it, thus far, so suppose it.

"The portion of the skull remaining is the left upper jaw. The teeth, judging from the apertures, must have been as large as those of an ox. It has a tusk projection from the back teeth, five inches long; on the whole it is quite a curiosity."

The correspondent who reported the story was Charles D. Evans of Springville, who also stated that the item was in his possession. The discovery is intriguing, but unfortunately, no one seems to know what became of the skull.

English traveler and writer Phil Robinson visited Utah in the 1880s and probed into the accounts. He wrote about the lake's monster in his book *Sinners and Saints*, stating:

"The Utah Lake has borne an uncomfortable reputation as the domain of strange water-apparitions. I would commend to notice the great snake of the Utah Lake. It has frightened men— and, far better evidence than that, it has been seen by children when playing on the shore. I say 'better,' because children are not likely to invent a plausible horror in order to explain their sudden rushing away from a given spot with terrified countenances and a consistent narrative."

The children that Robinson refers to are two boys he interviewed about their encounter with the creature.

Willie Roberts and George Scott were in a boat on the lake when they spotted what they first thought was a dog or a beaver in the water. The creature swam toward the boys, rose out of the water and issued a sound like the roar of a lion. The boys saw that the creature had four legs that were a yard long. They fled the scene and the monster pursued them. They managed to escape and reported the incident to their parents.

Robinson believed the boys had encountered an unknown creature and, in his writing, he questioned whether or not the Smithsonian was aware of the terrible monster.

The monster at Utah Lake never picked up the kind of steam that its counterpart at Bear Lake did and the few accounts quickly dwindled. Scant accounts in the following years were often explainable. One curious report did turn up in an article for *Utah Stories* magazine (October 13, 2017). Danny B. Stewart recalls a tale related to him by a friend in 2000. Stewart reports:

"James Chase noticed something strange swimming in the lake near Pelican Point. He was about forty yards away from it. He claimed to have seen something that was a little larger than a 'barrel drum' in width surface like a whale and then submerge again, He said it was 'shimmering silver in color with large yellow stripes running vertically along its mid-section.' James is a Hawaiian transplant and had encountered many different forms of ocean life, but he said he had 'never seen anything like this.'"

PART FOUR
Mysteries of the Great Salt Lake

The Great Salt Lake

A Strange and Curious Place

Approaching the Great Salt Lake, one gets the sense of an otherworldliness that is hard to express in words. Located in Northern Utah and sitting at an elevation of 4,206 feet, the lake appears like a mirage in the desert, surrounded by uninhabited mountain peaks and the barren salt flats. It's the largest remnant of the Pleistocene Epoch Lake Bonneville, a body of water that once covered over 22,000 square miles. The Great Salt Lake now covers an area of roughly 1,700 square miles, big enough to have an effect on weather in the region.

The Great Salt Lake is the largest saltwater lake in the Western Hemisphere. Its size fluctuates due primarily to the effects of evaporation on its shallow waters. The maximum depth is only around thirty-three feet.

The lake's high salt content causes swimmers to easily float on the water's surface, but the water is not a place that thrives with life. It's been called "America's Dead Sea" with good reason. While there are plenty of fish species that live and thrive in the surrounding and incoming waterways and marshes, the lake itself is not conducive to many species. In fact, the unusually high-level salinity makes the lake inhospitable to almost all forms of life. The exception is a small crustacean called the brine shrimp. The creatures are barely half an inch long and have transparent bodies. There are so many brine shrimp in the Great Salt Lake that it accounts for about ninety percent of the market and the creatures are shipped all over the world, They are primarily used in the aquarium trade and as food at prawn farms in Asia.

There are a couple of things you'll notice if you visit the Great Salt Lake. One is the stench. It is, at times, overpowering and is one of the biggest reasons that attempts to build a resort at the lakeside have never succeeded. The foul smell comes from a number of sources: the rotting bodies of brine shrimp, decomposing algae, and dead fish that have washed into the lake and perished—all being baked by the desert sun and giving off a stomach-turning sulfur-like odor.

There's something else you'll frequently encounter at the Great Salt Lake. Large black masses floating in the air. Some are disturbed to discover that these black clouds are actually swarms of brine flies.

There have long been strange stories associated with the lake. Early explorers were quite puzzled by it. Some thought the lake was part of the Pacific Ocean, or that it was connected to the ocean by underwater tunnels.

Native Americans in the region told tales of a tribe that lived on the islands in the Great Salt Lake. They were said to be a lost tribe of "white Indians."

They weren't the only denizens of the area. Tiny horses the size of dogs were once said to roam about the shores of the lake, as were creatures called salt bears who had an uncanny ability to camouflage themselves so that only their black eyes could be seen.

Some believe the ghostly bears still exist, terrorizing people driving alone on lonely stretches of highway in the region.

Reportedly, camels were once in the area around the lake. These sightings likely go back to the brief existence of the American Camel Corps, a short-lived attempt by the military to utilize camels in the deserts of the southwest in the 1800s. The camels were turned loose, and for years, there were sightings of the animals from Arizona to California.

Native legends spoke of a monster at the lake that would emerge from the water and snatch animals as large as horses and cows.

They also reported something that looked like a giant mosquito that preyed on man and animal alike. The creature would sweep down from the sky and suck the blood from its victims.

In the 1840s, a man called Brother Bainbridge reportedly spotted a creature that looked like a dolphin in the water near Antelope Island.

In the 1800s, there were various schemes hatched to stock the Great Salt Lake with creatures that could later be harvested. Several types of fish, oysters and crabs were all attempted, but none of them could survive the extreme salinity levels of the water.

Reportedly, the lake has "underwater quicksand" that will quickly pull in anyone unfortunate enough to tread upon it. There are numerous stories told about these dreadful traps. Supposedly, in the late 1930s, a man lost six of his horses after they left a sandbar and entered shallow water near Fremont Island. The horses were sucked down in a flash. There are also tales of herds of cattle being lost in similar fashion.

Early explorers reported that toxic fumes sometimes came out of nowhere at the lake. The fumes were said to be so deadly that they could instantly kill any man or beast who found themselves in the cloud and breathed them in.

Enjoying the Great Salt Lake circa 1904

Officials don't seem to put stock in the legends of toxic clouds or underwater quicksand, but one weird manifestation at the lake had more documentation. In 1966, a strange floating mass was reported. It first appeared in the south arm of the lake at a depth of twenty-two feet.

The mass was eight feet thick and looked like oozing slime. It also emitted a horrible odor that many said was reminiscent of rotten eggs.

The disturbing mass, whatever it was, stuck around. In 1969 the Utah Mineralogical and Geological Survey took a core sample from it hoping to learn what it was. The mass of slime was said to have the consistency of a "roll of baker's dough ready for the oven."

Many people assumed that the disgusting substance was an unusually large mass of brine fly larvae. The idea may sound far-fetched, but early explorer John C. Fremont reportedly saw a mass of larvae at the lake that was between ten and twenty feet wide.

Others opined that the mass was something equally unsettling—pickled raw sewage. Prior to the 1950s, dumping sewage in the lake was common practice. Even today, in some areas of the lake, there's a layer of sludge at the bottom. Leftover, perhaps, from a time when people just didn't know any better.

Despite official inquiries, no one ever really provided a satisfactory answer to explain the oozing mass that floated on the lake. To make the whole matter stranger, the mass mysteriously disappeared in 1991.

Perhaps the question we should be asking is—where is it now?

With its high level of salinity, one of the last things you would expect in the Great Salt Lake are icebergs, but they have, on occasion, shown up.

In 1942, a massive iceberg formed in the lake. It was reported to be 30 feet high and around 100 feet across. In 1984 several icebergs showed up during a winter freeze.

Unique conditions must come into play for icebergs to form in the lake. In short, this occurs when an area of freshwater becomes trapped over the lake's saline water. When atmospheric conditions are right, the water can freeze and form into a layer of ice. The layer, in turn, can break up and form a floating iceberg.

Beyond these curiosities, there have been a few monster tales from the Great Salt Lake. In *Folklore in the Bear Lake Valley*, Bonnie Thompson reports that a creature was reportedly caught in the lake and put on display for a brief time in 1871. The creature was exhibited for a time at a resort in the Black Rock area. A group of scientists came to examine the carcass and discovered that it was in reality an immense codfish that had been shipped in from the east coast. Eight chicken legs had been attached to the fish to create the so-called monster.

Six years later, another monster story surfaced. According to the July 14, 1877, edition of the *Salt Lake Semi-Weekly Herald*, the night workers at Barnes and Company's Salt Works, located at Monument Point near Kelton, heard weird noises coming from the lake. Investigating the sound, they saw a "huge mass of hide and fin rapidly approaching the shore towards the camp."

One of the witnesses, J.H. McNiel, said the creature looked like a crocodile or alligator but "must have been seventy-five feet long; but the head was not like an alligator's; it was more like a horse's."

When it was almost at the shore, the creature raised its head and issued a "terrible bellow."

The frightened men fled the scene, rushing up into the mountains where they spent a restless night in the rocks.

The following morning, the group returned to their site and found their camp torn up. Large tracks were found along the shore where the creature had been seen but there was no other evidence of the beast.

McNiel reportedly signed an affidavit before Kelton's Justice of the Peace as a testimony of the veracity of the account.

After the sighting hit the papers, another encounter surfaced. Reportedly, a few years prior, Judge Dennis J. Toohy had a run-in with the creature.

Toohy was swimming in the lake early one morning. He was about a half a mile out when there was commotion in the water. The judge's first thought was that it was due to one of the mysterious underwater tunnels said to exist in the lake. Concerned for his safety, lest he be swept to his death in a watery passage, Toohy turned back to shore.

Around a hundred yards from shore, the judge stood up and looked around. He was shocked to see, about 200 yards from his position, the outline of a large creature. The beast was moving slowly, presumably due to the shallow water, and its large tail thrashed about, causing waves to move across the lake.

Toohy rushed to dry land, retrieved his clothing, and headed back to the city. He related the story to a few close friends and together they returned to the lake to look for the creature. They found tracks along the shore, similar to those reported at Monument Point. The judge kept his encounter quiet until the report from the McNiel party.

Whale Tales

In the 1800s, a man by the name of James Wickham had what he thought was a brilliant idea. He wanted to import whales to populate the Great Salt Lake. Wickham was confident that the ocean giants could survive the lake's intense salt waters.

Allegedly, Wickham spent a year in Australia during which time he captured a pair of whales. The creatures were placed in a ship that had a specially designed hold to transport them safely across the ocean to the United States.

Wickham and his whales docked in San Francisco in 1873 and from there, the creatures were transported in giant tanks via train to Utah.

Purportedly, the two whales were 35 feet long. Once they arrived in the Beehive State, they were placed in custom pens at the mouth of the Bear River prior to being released into the Great Salt Lake.

The whales escaped the pen, smashing their way through the enclosure, and vanishing into the lake which is where Wickham said he wanted them anyway.

Once they were in the lake, they couldn't be located. People soon assumed that the whales had died in the lake, unable to survive the unusual environment. However, six months after their escape, the animals were reportedly spotted.

If we are to believe the account, the missing six months had been good for the pair. They had both grown to sixty feet in length and had several smaller whales with them, presumably offspring, that ranged from three to fifteen feet in length.

The July 22, 1956, edition of the *Salt Lake Tribune* recalled the outrageous tale:

"The agent followed the whales for five successive days and nights. Discovering that the original pair are now sixty feet in length and followed about by a school of several hundred young, varying in length from three to fifteen feet. The scheme is a surprising and complete success and Mr. Wickham has earned the thanks of mankind."

Purportedly, the whales thrived for a time in the lake, but things took another turn when whalers found out about the animals. Hungry for profit and easy targets, the whalers came in and hunted the creatures to extinction.

So we're told.

Despite there being numerous issues with the tale, the crazy story of the Great Salt Lake whales has circulated for a long time and has become part of the folklore of the lake. The University of Utah's department of biology even mentioned the whale story on their website, noting:

"Though there have been several alleged whale sightings, scientists believe that they could not have survived the lake's high salt content."

The tale has circulated for so long that, in 1995, the *Deseret News* tried to find evidence of the Great Salt Lake whales. Representatives from the paper did a thorough search but could find no valid source to verify the story.

Another whale of a story turned up in 2014. According to a December 5 report, a dairy farmer in the town of Farmington found a whale carcass in his field.

69-year-old farmer Michael Woodson was out looking for one of his missing cows when he discovered the massive carcass of a humpback whale on his property.

Woodson couldn't understand how a whale had ended up in his field and the police department was called to investigate the matter. The account claimed that a team of biologists from the University of Utah were also summoned to examine the whale.

"We have to admit that we find this case very puzzling," reported Farmington police captain Terry Dawson.

The story was posted and reposted at various sites, causing concerned citizens to call Davis County dispatch and the local Fox 13 newsroom.

Once the original source of the story was discovered—*World News Daily Report*—the matter was resolved. The *Daily* is a satirical "news" site, and the entire whale tale was fabricated.

BEEHIVE STATE MONSTERS by David Weatherly

Outrageous Monsters

In the early 1900s there were some rather absurd monster stories related to the Great Salt Lake that ran in newspapers around the country. Although it's clear the creatures in question weren't real, I present these accounts here for those interested in the historic and folkloric aspects of cryptid legends.

Pennsylvania's *The Star* published a lengthy story in its January 6, 1904, edition about a purported encounter with a bizarre creature with direct "testimony" from the men who claimed to see it:

"Combination of Fish, Alligator and Bat Found

"A terrible, nameless, unclassified creature of the animal world is exciting the curiosity, wonder and fear of occasional visitors to Stansbury Island, in the southern portion of Great Salt Lake.

"This monster, for it can be called nothing else, has lately, it is said, been seen by several persons, but the best account of its characteristics and movements is given by Martin Gilbert and John Barry, two hunters who this week returned from an expedition over the island, in the course of which they studied the habits of this hitherto unheard-of creature for three days.

"The monster, which appears to be almost equally at home in the air, on the beach, or submerged in the briny waters of Salt Lake, is probably the sole survivor of a prehistoric species. It is doubtless the last representative of a family whose other members, dead ages since, have left the testimony of their existence in the primeval rocks of the mountains.

"Arranging in concise form the description of this incredible relic of the animal world, from the accounts given by those who have observed it at close range, it seems in plain, unscientific language a combination of fish, alligator, and bat.

"Description of the Beast

"In size it is simply tremendous. Gilbert places its length at 50 feet, while Barry, who is an amateur scientist, says that an examination of its tracks demonstrates that the monster must be at least 65 feet from head to tail.

"The head is like that of an alligator, the eyes fiercely glowing; the jaws, capable of opening to a distance of 10 feet from the top of the upper to the lower, are provided with a fearful array of sharp saw-edged teeth; the body, so far as observations goes, is increased with heavy, horny scales. As to this Gilbert and Barry are not positive, as the constant diving of the beast, if such it may be called, into the strong brine of the lake has incrusted it with a thick coating of salt, which save near the wings completely hides the body.

"According to their account they first sighted it at a distance of between one and a half and two miles. The day was clear, the sun intensely bright. Gilbert's own words of discoverery are:

"'We were walking westward from the east shore of the island about 9 o'clock in the morning when suddenly to the northwest there appeared a thing. I don't know what to call it. It looked to me like a brilliant rainbow folded into compact mass, moving rapidly through the air.'

"'I was so astounded that for a few moments I doubted the evidence of my own senses. The object came nearer, but the colors were so dazzling that it was some time before it assumed definite form. No one who has not witnessed the sight can conceive its strangeness. The mass of color was glowing, flaming, radiant. I spoke to Barry, saying:

"'For God's sake, man, can you see that?' and he was no less astonished than myself.'

"'In three or four minutes the monster's position was such that it no longer reflected the sunlight directly toward us, and we would then discern the outline of the form. Its wings were bat-like, stretching out over a great expanse. I should say at least 100 feet from tip to tip. The tail was proportionately short, and resembled that of a huge fish. We were not close enough at this time to tell much about the head, only we saw that the jaws were very long. In shape the head was like that of a crocodile.'

"Gilbert gave a long account of how he and Barry watched the monster, which supported its enormous wings, swung round and round in immense circles through the air, gradually descending and approaching nearer to them. He declares that it was not more than 300 yards above their heads, when, now convinced that the awful creature was about to attack them, he fired at the monster with his rifle, a 44-calibre gun loaded with a steel cased bullet.

"The missile, he believes, struck fair, but inflicted no apparent wound. The monster gave utterance to a strange, fear-inspiring cry, half snort, half roar, and, rising rapidly in the air, veered quickly to the west, and after three miles of flight settled down and disappeared beyond the crest of the hills.

Bullet Had No Effect

"A few seconds after the shot was fired, while the hunters were watching the flight of the dragon-like beast, some small lumps of salt fell almost at their feet. They were more than ever mystified by this, but not until the next day were they able to ascertain its source.

"Determined to learn more of the monster, Gilbert and Barry hastened in the direction of its flight, and after surmounting the range of hills to the westward, found with little trouble the tracks the beast had left in the soil after ceasing its flight. These led the hunters to an immense cave, near the head of a narrow gulch.

"They approached to within three rods of the opening in the rocks but finding that the freshest footprints led into the gloomy cavern, feared at that time to make any closer inspection.

"'These tracks,' said Barry, 'were five-toed, almost exactly like the imprint of a gigantic hand, if you can imagine a hand nearly four feet across the palm.'

"Gilbert and Barry constructed a barricade for themselves of the largest rocks they were able to handle and lay down to await the results.

"The day wore on and the men were weary and almost despairing of success in their vigil, when, just at dusk, the horrible creature crawled slowly from the cave, and, pausing at its mouth to take flight, gave them their first view at close range."

Barry says that the hackneyed phrase of exaggeration, "made his blood run cold," is none too strong for the sight they saw.

"'The monster slowly moved his great jaws,' declared the hunter, in speaking of his experience, 'until it seemed as if he could have swallowed a large horse in one mouthful. He gave a snort that might have been heard a mile, and then slowly spread his huge wings. We now saw that the huge body was coated with salt, apparently nearly a foot in thickness. This explained why the salt lumps dropped at our feet when the bullet struck the monster. By this we knew that the creature must spend much of its time in the waters of the lake.

"'The great beast made a short run before taking flight, taking long jumps upon its hind legs and tail. The forelegs were comparatively short and appeared to be used only when it crawled flat upon the ground.

"'The frightful head was not more than ten feet from us when it rose in the air, but so well were we screened by our shelter of rocks that we were unobserved. The large, fiercely gleaming eyes, the sharp serrated teeth, the wide expanse of wings that began to move rapidly as the horrible beast rose from the ground and passed directly over our heads, combined to make a terrible sight—one that I shall never forget.

"'We watched it disappear in the gathering gloom of night, but were for a long time paralyzed with fear, not knowing when it might return. It was probably an hour later when it did come back.

"'We heard the swish of the mighty wings before it could be seen, but as it drew nearer, by the light of the young moon in the West, we saw that it carried in its great jaws a large horse, which I supposed it had swooped down upon while feeding. The horse was badly crushed and mangled.

Feasted on the Horse

"'The monster carried its burden into the cave, and we could hear the crunching of its jaws and the cracking of the horse's bones as the beast devoured its victim. After an hour or so all was so still, and then slipped quietly away in the darkness and returned to our camp on the eastern shore of the island.

"'Had it not been for a bad break in our boat we would have fled the island that night. As it was, we worked all night to repair the craft, although the task might have been accomplished in two hours except that we feared to build a fire to afford light.

"'It was just dawn, and we were preparing to launch, when Gilbert said: "There it comes again!" In an instant we turned the boat bottom up and crawled under it. One end was lifted about a foot above the end by a rock, and we were able to watch the monster's actions.

"'It settled down on the beach less than fifty yards to the north and dived quickly into the lake. From its actions while nearly buried under the waves I judged that the creature was gathering and feeding upon the saltwater shrimps which abound along the coast there. When the monster came up it was very close to us, and we were particularly impressed by the fact that the strong brine had no effect upon its eyes, which appeared lidless. Evidently the animal's food in the water was found by the sense of sight.

"'Although of such gigantic size, there was nothing sluggish in the movements of the monster. It swam and dived as rapidly as any large fish.

"'We watched it for perhaps half an hour as it gradually worked its way northward and finally disappeared.'"

The September 9, 1906, edition of the *Los Angeles Herald* carried the full, absurd story of another monster; this one was supposedly captured at the Great Salt Lake. The story ran under the banner "Man Captures a Strange Animal."

"Murray, Utah, Sept 8—James Franson of this village recently made one of the most remarkable discoveries of the century—one which will keep the learned men busy for months to come in explaining what they have always declared was an impossibility, namely, that no living thing could exist in the salty waters of the inland sea—Great Salt Lake.

"Until a week ago Mr. Franson was of the same opinion as the professors who have written so much about the briny waters of the lake, but today you couldn't make him believe that any animal resembling a cross between a monster fish and an alligator does not thrive where nothing else can sustain life.

"Mr. Franson's discovery came about in this way: While camped on Antelope Island one day last week, Franson, his wife and two sons were sitting on the shore of the lake. While they were looking out across the water toward Salt Lake City the father beheld an animal swimming lazily on the surface of the lake and not more than 100 feet from shore. Without taking his eyes from the spot he called to his wife and sons to look where he was pointing.

"As they did so the queer looking object raised itself from the water and sent forth a shriek that was the nearest approach to the wail of a human being that could be imagined. As the terrifying sound ceased, the animal dropped back into the water and continued its journey toward the shore.

"Almost instantly the Fransons were again startled to see several smaller members of the same family swimming ten or fifteen feet behind the great Salt Lake monster.

Captures Strange Saurian

"For a few seconds the Murrayites kept their eyes on the strange appearing group of animals (or whatever you are pleased to call them), but as the importance of the discovery revealed itself to the elder Franson he jumped to his feet and set about to effect a capture.

"In his early days, as everyone hereabout knows, Mr. Franson was one of the beast steer punchers that Montana boasted, and quick as a flash he ran to the camp and then returned with a rope some fifty feet in length and prepared to take a try at lassoing the strange animal.

"By this time, it had approached to within twenty feet of the shore, closely followed by the smaller members of its family.

"Circling the rope above his head, Franson made a swift and accurate throw and caught the wriggling monster about two feet below its head. Then, like a flash, he made a half hitch of the other end of the rope around a limb of a tree and the capture was complete.

"For fully an hour the monster wriggled and twisted, straining so hard at times that Franson feared the half inch rope would be snapped, but slowly the animal lost its strength and eventually was hauled ashore.

"By actual measurement the monster was thirty-three feet long. Its head resembled that of an alligator, but the tail and body were of a slate-colored hue, and it looked more like a man-eating shark than anything else.

"After securing the 'fish-alligator' with other ropes and making sure that it could not escape, Franson got into his launch and made a hasty trip to Saltair and thence to Salt Lake City, where several well-known men who knew Franson would not concoct such a story for the purpose of playing a joke on them were induced to return with him and transport the monster to Salt Lake.

"Taken to Saltair

"The trip was naturally a dangerous one, for the instant that the monster recovered its strength it lashed the water into a white foam and more than once succeeded in taking the launch a mile or more out of its course.

"A huge tank was secured at Saltair and eventually the strange monster was landed in the Salt Palace, where a special aquarium was erected for its home.

"The palace has been crowded with visitors every day since the doors were thrown open to the public; more than 10,000 people having already paid 25 cents each to behold the only animal of its kind every captured, and, so far as known, the only one (with the exception of the other members of the same family which promptly disappeared when Franson lassoed the mother) that has ever been seen.

"As the waters of Salt Lake are more than one-third salt it seems impossible that anything could live in it, but the evidence furnished by Mr. Franson is indisputable.

"What seems all the more remarkable concerning the monster is that it comes nearer imitating the human voice than a parrot. Many who have watched the gigantic 'fish-alligator' declare that it all but talks, and the attendant who never leaves the Salt Palace goes further and declares it does talk.

"'I don't care how much fun you make of me,' he said the other day, 'that thing can talk as plainly as a man can, for I have heard it say things when there was no one but myself anywhere near the building. Why, just last night, shortly after the doors had been locked and I was preparing to go to bed, that great whale of a fish raised its head out of the water and said:

"'Say Bill, what has become of my old friend Brigham Young? I heard indirectly that he was dead.'

"The attendant also declares that the monster can sing, and he would not be much surprised if some enterprising theatrical manager tried to secure it as an attraction. The attendant has figured it out that the blamed thing could even be taught to play piano, there seemingly being no limit to its powers of imitating the human voice and doing what it sees or hears human beings doing. Scientists from Brigham Junction declare that the monster is 44,000 years old at least, and possibly older."

5

PART FIVE
Legends of Deseret

BEEHIVE STATE MONSTERS by David Weatherly

Strange Things in the Sky

The *Ogden Standard-Examiner* reported an incident in its July 23, 1894, edition involving a giant, flying serpent. Reportedly, a group of "reliable men" watched the 100-foot-long serpent as it soared over the town of Eden in Weber County. The beast swooped down near Wilbur's Store and over the town park. It was flying at an estimated 35 to 40 miles per hour. The thing then headed toward the mountains and vanished, never to be seen again.

Around 1738, a group of Spanish soldiers were hauling a load of silver ingots out of Utah. The Spanish had been mining in the region for some time and had angered the local Utes who considered the territory their hunting grounds.

The Spaniards were attacked and most of them killed. Amidst the chaos, two men managed to survive by hiding behind some rocks. They watched as the rest of their party was slaughtered. The natives then took the burros into a nearby cave and killed the animals. Accounts say the cave had a petroglyph of a large, strange bird over its entrance.

The men reported the slaughter, and their testimony was recorded in church records. Spanish authorities considered sending more soldiers back for the silver, but ultimately decided it wasn't worth the trouble and the treasure was abandoned. The story became another Utah treasure legend passed down through the years.

Writing in *Unsolved Mysteries of the Old West*, W. C. Jameson reports on an interesting discovery made by a treasure hunter in the 1980s. The man had launched a long search for the legendary Thunderbird cave and had scoured the region looking for the lost silver. He finally located the spot and the petroglyph of the large, winged creature that the Spanish survivors had reported.

The cave contained a thick layer of dust and sand and he started the tedious work of removing the material in his search for the silver. Eventually, he unearthed burro hooves, an indication that at least part of the legend was true. Even more intriguing, he found an unusual feather. Jameson reports:

"The shaft of the feather, though broken, was just over eighteen inches long and the base, as feathers go, was as big around as one of his fingers. The treasure hunter had considerable experience with eagles and hawks and was very familiar with their feathers, but this one was several times larger than any he had ever seen before. The soft barbs that extended from the shaft, had, for the most part, rotted away, but enough of the structure remained such that it was unmistakably a feather of an incredibly large bird."

Reportedly, ornithologists confirmed that the feather was from a bird's wing, though they could not determine what kind of bird.

Some speculate that the natives sacrificed the burros to a giant, winged creature that lived in the cave, perhaps to placate it or perhaps to employ it as a guardian over the silver.

As expected, the treasure hunter kept the location of the cave a secret and it's unclear who currently has possession of the unusual bird feather.

Another giant bird mystery arose in the state in 1936 when explorers found what they believed were giant bird nests in the desert near the Great Salt Lake. The Winter 1960 edition of western magazine *Frontier Times* ran a story about the find under the headline "A New Mystery on the Donner Trail."

"Nowhere in the world is there a wilderness so desolate, so untraveled as Utah's Mud Desert. Barren, completely without vegetation, and so level the distant horizon is a burning white glare at the rim of the world, the Mud Desert is mysterious and dangerous, a challenge to man's physical and intellectual resources.

"Only two groups of travelers are known to have crossed the Mud Desert which is part of the great area loosely defined as The Great Salt Desert. The first was the tragedy bound Donner

Party, migrating to California in 1850. Eighty-six years later, Dr. Walter M. Stookey successfully followed the Donner route and emerged from his experience in the wilderness with some of the most surprising discoveries ever to be made in the Desert State."

The article goes on to describe the journey that Stookey and his party took as they retraced the steps of the doomed Donner party. Stookey and his men found items discarded by the Donner group that included clothing, furniture, and wagon parts. As they continued through the desert, they found more items including "great quantities of clothing, unopened trunks, beds and the skeletons of many oxen." Stookey also found an unmarked desert cemetery for some of the party that had died on the route. Some of the items were collected and later donated to the University of Utah Museum.

While disturbing, many of the finds were likely expected since the fate of the Donner party was well known. What Stookey didn't expect was his next find. According to the article:

"While following the trail and after entering the most desolate part of the Mud Desert, Stookey and his companions stumbled upon some huge mounds. Some of them were six to eight feet high and resembled gigantic bird nests. Limited by time and the necessity to proceed, the adventurers did not pause for a thorough investigation. Stookey, however, could not get the bird nests off his mind. He did a lot of digging into Indian myths and read many accounts of trappers, explorers, and trail-crossers, and the following year he went back specifically to inspect the strange phenomena."

Reportedly, a publication named *The Pony Express* out of Sonora, California, ran a story about the nests and attributed them to "Behemoth Bannock Birds," a species the publication said was long extinct but were "leviathans of prehistoric times that outlived their other companions of dinosaur days and existed until less than 150 years ago."

The publication claimed to have proof of the existence of the birds but did not offer any evidence.

Reportedly, the Behemoth Bannock Birds were five times larger than modern eagles and preyed on large animals such as deer, antelope, and mountain sheep which they could easily carry off to their nests.

Stookey is said to have found items from the Donner

party in some of the nests that he discovered, giving the creepy implication that some of the party may have been caught by giant raptors. Of course, there's never been any indication that such a thing occurred, and the deaths of the Donner party are well documented at this point.

Scientists from the University of Utah believe the nests were built by the rough-legged hawk. The explanation may be a rational one, but the experts fail to explain why the nests would be so large. They also seem to ignore the fact that there are no other locations where the hawks have built such nests, nor were any members of the species found using the nests discovered by Stookey.

Some people have speculated that the "nests" were nothing but natural formations that Stookey mistook for bird nests, but this idea has also been disputed.

Fortean researcher Theo Paijmans notes that the subject was discussed in 1943 at the annual meeting of the sciences, arts and letters held at the Utah State Agricultural College where Dr. William H. Behle, Dr. Woodbury, and Dr. W.P. Cottam of the University of Utah presented *Further Light on the 'Fossil' Bird Nests of the Great Salt Lake Desert*.

If the nests weren't made by hawks, then where did they come from? Some people believe the answer was discovered in 2006 when scientists revealed the discovery of an ancient creature.

"Scientists from the University of Utah and the Utah Museum of Natural History have discovered the remains of a new bird-like, meat-eating dinosaur in Grand Staircase-Escalante National Monument, southern Utah. The new dinosaur was formally named Hagryphus giganteus, which means "giant four-footed, bird-like god of the western desert" in reference to the animal's outward resemblance to a large land bird, its gigantic stature, and its discovery in the Utah desert."

A paper about the discovery of the creature was published in the *Journal of Vertebrate Paleontology* (Volume 25 Issue 4). The bird-like dinosaur was around seven feet tall, had a strong, toothless beak, powerful arms and claws, and could run up to twenty-five miles per hour.

The creature certainly sounds creepy enough and could have been carried through native oral tradition as a cultural memory from a period when tribal members coexisted with large, now extinct creatures.

Such tales could also explain stories of the "Great Mosquito Monster" that was said to dwell around the Great Salt Lake.

On July 18, 1966, news reports said that residents of Salt Lake City were on the lookout for a giant bird seen flying over the east bench area. Several people thought it might be an eagle, but others disagreed. A witness named C.L. Fairbanks reportedly spotted the creature and said that it was "about as big as a Piper Cub airplane." The bird circled briefly, then flew off in an easterly direction. The *Deseret News* jokingly reported that it "could be Batman."

A report on the *Utah UFO Hunters* website describes a weird, winged entity spotted in the southern portion of the state near the town of Panguitch, Garfield County, in the summer of 1976.

The witnesses were driving north on State Road 89 in the Dixie National Forest. It was around eleven o'clock at night and they were in a lightly forested area. They had their high beams on, and the lights picked up a strange figure in a clearing about seventy feet away. It was reportedly half man and half bird. The witness described the creature as:

"About 5 ½ ft tall to 6 ft tall, it had large eyes that did not glow or produce any color, a large head, and no visible neck. It had wings that were either folded or attached to the front. There were visible feathers and the skin looked like weathered, human looking skin with dark or dirty spots on it. It had a wide body that seemed to accommodate its wings."

The driver slowed down as they moved past the creature. The witness turned the vehicle around to get a better look at the thing, but it had vanished.

Researcher Albert Rosales has an account from mid-2009 from a couple who spotted a large, winged creature near Provo.

The witness reported:

"I thought I could see a rounded, long beak/nose and a giant body. I would maybe compare it to a bat or a pterodactyl, I didn't see any feathers. It was hard to tell because it was kind of shadowy, I guess is what I would describe it as. Or blurry, like it was blending in with the sky or surroundings. But it wasn't invisible, it was just hard to see the details."

The creature was "grayish brown, dark, maybe black," which added to the camouflage effect. The couple was on the porch of their trailer around 6 a.m. when they observed the creature. They first thought they were observing a plane, but quickly realized it was something alive. The size was close to that of a crop duster or slightly smaller. The wings were bat-like, and no feathers were noted. The witness adds:

"The strangest thing about it was how it flew. It looked like it was swimming through the sky, kind of gliding. It undulated through the sky, and I think it was going pretty fast, although the way it seemed to just swim through the sky made it look like it was going slow."

Old Ephraim

Although you won't find any grizzly bears roaming around the Beehive State, at least not officially, they did once call the area home and one large specimen left behind quite a legend.

The bear was sometimes known as "Old Three Toes," a nicknamed he earned due to one of his feet having only three toes. He's commonly remembered today as "Old Ephraim."

The legendary bear reportedly stood ten feet tall when on his hind legs and he was said to have weighed more than half a ton. Legend claims he could bite a six-inch aspen limb in half with one snap of his powerful jaws.

In the early 1900s, Old Ephraim terrorized farms and ranches in the Cache Valley, taking farm animals at will. The poor sheep proved easy pickings for a large grizzly, and the ranchers were, of course, irritated at losing their animals to the beast.

Ephraim's reign of terror ended on August 22, 1923. That's when the giant grizzly met his match in the form of a man named Frank Clark. Clark arrived in the valley in 1911 and went to work as a sheepherder. He says that in his first season alone, bears killed 154 adult sheep.

By 1913, Clark was actively trapping bears and that year alone he caught thirteen, but his main target, the giant Old Ephraim, eluded him for a long time. The hunter tried numerous times to trap the giant bear, but it was so smart that it would remove traps without setting them off.

Clark chased Old Ephraim for twelve years before the final encounter. The hunter was camped in Logan Canyon and had set traps around his camp. He was awakened by a roar and when he went to find the source of the noise, he discovered the grizzly caught in one of the traps. A fourteen-foot chain was wrapped around the animal's right forelimb and a twenty-three-pound bear trap was stuck on the bear's paw.

Clark's account of his pursuit and killing of Old Ephraim is on file at the Utah State University Archives under the title "True Bear Story as Told by Frank Clark, Malad, Idaho" In it, he gives details of the bear's end:

"Ephraim raised up on his hind legs with his back to me and a 14-foot long chain wound around his right arm as carefully as a man would have done it and a 23-pound bear trap on his foot and standing 9 feet 11 inches high."

"I was paralyzed with fear and couldn't raise my gun and he was coming, still on his hind legs, holding that cussed trap above his head. He had a four-foot bank to surmount before he could reach me. I was rooted to the earth and let him come withing six feet of me before I stuck the gun out and pulled the trigger.

"He fell back but came again and received five of the remaining six bullets. He had now reached the trail, still on his hind legs. I only had one cartridge left in the gun and still that bear wouldn't go down, so I started for Logan, 20 miles downhill."

As Clark fled, the bear pursued, still on his hind legs. Clark's dog leapt in and started snapping at Ephraim, and Clark turned back on the bear, this time, seeing clearly how badly hurt the creature was. Blood was spouting from Ephraim's nostrils, and he was having difficulty breathing. Clark got closer and used his last bullet to finally bring the bear down.

Clark says that he was a lover of nature, and as a result, never hunted until he saw how much damage bears were doing in the area; he became set on tracking them down, especially Old Ephraim.

Clark reports that the bear was named by sheepherders in the region who had read about a similar grizzly in California in a book by P.T. Barnum.

Clark took the bear's hide as a trophy, buried the creature

where he'd killed it, then headed home to tell his story.

A few months later, a troop of Boy Scouts dug the bear's carcass up and took the skull. They sold it to the Smithsonian Institution in Washington D.C. for a grand total of twenty-five dollars.

The Smithsonian later loaned the skull to the Utah State University in Logan where it was put on display in the campus library.

Clark claimed that he saw another massive grizzly near Logan in 1936, stating, "I also saw a grizzly bear eating a lamb on August 31, 1936, but had no gun. Saw his tracks again in 1941."

There's no further documentation on the sighting and Old Ephraim became known as the last of Utah's grizzlies.

In 1966, a troop of Boy Scouts dedicated an eleven-foot-high stone monument to the legendary grizzly. The monument is at the bear's gravesite about nine miles up Logan Canyon.

The monument has a poem engraved at its base, written by Nephi J. Bott. It reads:

Old Ephraim, old Ephraim, your deeds were so wrong

Yet we build you this marker and sing you this song.

To the king of the forest so mighty and tall,

We salute you old Ephraim the king of them all.

Phantom Kangaroos

So-called "phantom kangaroos" have plagued areas of several states over the years from the Midwest, down to Oklahoma, and yes, they've even shown up in Utah.

The marsupials are usually described as being 3 ½ to 6 feet tall and are generally described as "regular kangaroos." Additional, strange qualities are sometimes noted, however, including glowing eyes.

A rogue kangaroo was reportedly wandering around Cedar Fort in the summer of 1981. Rancher Ray Ault contacted officials at the Hogle Zoo hoping to find the source of the out-of-place marsupial. Ault had spotted the animal amidst his sheep. He said the creature was yellowish in color with darker tones around its ears. As reported in Provo, UT's *Daily Herald* on June 12, 1981:

"Ault, who has been raising sheep in the desert range west of Utah Lake for 50 years, said he knew something was wrong when he saw an animal in his herd leap about six feet into the air.

"I was checking the sheep up the canyon, and off to the side of them I saw something jump straight up. I got closer to the animal, and it looked me right in the eye. Then jump... jump...jump...off it went."

Ault told several people about the sighting. His friends doubted him at first, likely thinking he'd been out in the summer sun a bit too long, but he stuck to the details of his story, and they finally believed him.

"I've seen kangaroos in the movies and on TV and there was no mistaking it. It looked like a giant kangaroo rat...Who knows where the thing came from?," Ault told reporters.

Ault and his friend Jim Davis contacted both the Hogle Zoo and Liberty Park in Salt Lake City to report the incident. Both locations were known to have kangaroos and Ault thought perhaps they had lost one of their marsupials. Both venues reported all their kangaroos present and accounted for, leaving Ault and his friends with a real mystery on their hands. How had a random kangaroo ended up in Utah's western desert, and why was it hanging out with Ault's sheep?

If the animal was an escapee from a zoo, it was one from well out of the region that was never reported.

There's always the possibility that it was an exotic pet that escaped and went on tour, stopping briefly among Ray Ault's sheep before going...somewhere.

Even weirder than the rancher's account is a purported cluster of sightings that occurred around the Southwest in the 1950s. Utah was among the states visited by creatures described as "screaming kangaroos." The animals were reportedly around four feet tall and weighed in the range of 150 pounds.

Many of the descriptions claimed the creatures had "powerful hind legs, stubby arms, and sharp teeth." Out of place kangaroos are one thing, but according to some of the reports, the animals also had "reptilian features and wings," AND they issued "bloodcurdling screams."

Kangaroos are, of course, endemic to the Australian continent, but one never knows. Utah has a lot of land and there could still be some large, jumping marsupials out there somewhere.

Phantom Kangaroos

Giant Snakes

Utah has its fair share of snakes of the known variety, including the non-venomous glossy snake, the night snake, and the common kingsnake. The state also harbors some deadly pit vipers including the sidewinder, the Mojave rattlesnake and the midget faced rattlesnake. Some of these specimens can reach several feet in length. A five-foot rattlesnake can certainly be an intimidating sight, but imagine a slithering serpent 10, 20 or more feet in length. Could such things possibly be wandering around the state?

In the early 1870s, the *Deseret Weekly News* reported on a couple of giant snake stories. The paper's July 30, 1873, edition started their report by first referencing an earlier account, one published in their September 3, 1862, edition. In that issue, a letter from a man in Spring Lake Villa told the story of a giant snake encountered by some native Americans in the mountains east of the city. According to the correspondent, a man and some women had gone to the mountain to pick berries but returned the following day in a disturbed state. For some time, the man would not reveal what had happened to him, but eventually he told the story. As the letter writer recounts:

"He went over the other side of the mountain, and then, after walking about a while came upon the trail of something appearing as though timber had been dragged along. This he crossed, and upon going a little higher, saw the head of some living thing peeping over a rock at him, which much frightened him, as he had never seen anything like it; but before he could run, a huge snake, as thick through as a man's body, and from ten to twenty feet long, sprang towards him. He dodged, and the huge reptile went clear over his head, but gathered himself up again, as the Indian started the other way, and again jumped. Another dodge saved him again, when he scrambled over some rocks and up the mountain, getting not only clear of his snakeship, but nearly frightened out of his senses. He says the snake had horns that curved back over his head, and that he would raise his head to the height of a man."

The writer assured the paper that the story was "generally believed" by those who knew the man while others had their doubts about the reported giant.

The paper used the story to segue into an account they had received involving a man named Edward R. Walker in 1873. Walker, the paper reported, was from Salt Lake City's 16th Ward, was thirty-four years old, and a stout, strong man accustomed to mountain life. Walker himself visited the paper and reported his encounter with a large serpent. The *News* reports:

"On the 16th instant Mr. Walker, his brother Sylvester, and their cousin John Coon, were felling timber for Mr. Standish's mill, in the righthand fork of Coon's Canyon, about three quarters of a mile from the Point of the mountain west from this city, on the high peak, south of Black Rock. Between ten and eleven in the morning, a deer ran by where they were working, and our informant snatched up a Sharp's rifle, and started in pursuit. When he had continued the chase for about a mile, due north, he was startled by a loud, shrill whistle and hiss, which he first thought might be a signal from an Indian. He came to a halt and looked about him and heard the noise of rocks rattling southeast from where he stood. He turned, when to his horror, he saw approaching him, at a very rapid rate, a serpent, which he judged was between thirty and forty feet long, and about ten inches through the body. The reptile's head was raised fully six feet from the ground, and his jaws were open fifteen or eighteen inches wide with large fangs growing from both upper and lower jaw.

"Walker was petrified with fear, but the hope of saving his own life made him start to run. The serpent, however, was too quick for him, and jumped at and knocked him down, striking him on the left shoulder just below the shoulder blade, going over him and down the mountain to the southwest for a short distance, when he turned and pursued Walker, who had risen and with speed inspired by the deadliest fear was making his way to the top of the ridge."

Walker stumbled and fell to the ground. Almost instantly, the serpent was on him, slithering over his body. Walker reports that he could feel the weight of the thing as it glided over him.

Either the snake didn't think Walker would make a good meal, or it was unsure what it was dealing with. Whatever the case, the reptile decided to retreat, taking off at a high rate of speed. The report continues:

"Walker rose and watched his movements, and says that after crossing to the east side, the snake turned and recrossed to the west side and went down the mountain a few yards, and then twined himself around a large mahogany tree where he remained waving his head to and fro, flapping his tail on the rocks, and whistling and hissing defiance."

Walker returned to his companions and reported the encounter. The other men were anxious to launch a hunt for the serpent, but Walker said he was "too weak from fright and excitement to do so."

Walker did report that the group intended to return to the mountain and try to locate the snake. He gave the paper the following description of the creature:

"The color of the reptile was yellow, with a black mark like a half moon on each side of his eyes; he had a beard or fuzz round his mouth, and what appeared to our informant to be a crown shaped mass on top of his head. The latter was about six inches high, and varied in color, being green, blue, white, yellow, and red. The head of the creature was about as large as that of a full-grown bulldog and in shape between that of a bulldog and a monkey. His body was covered with scales, six or eight inches long."

Walker said he had lived in the mountains for years and had never been afraid of anything he'd encountered. He did note, however, that he would never return to the fork of Coon's Canyon alone. He also showed reporters the large, bruised area on his shoulder where the snake had reportedly struck him and knocked him down.

The story involving Walker certainly sounds like a typical, embellished, or completely fabricated news item from the period with the elaborate description of the serpent resembling something more akin to a classical Asian dragon.

A brief report from 1893 that says a giant rattlesnake was killed near Salina in Sevier County. The snake reportedly measured a massive seventeen feet and had 164 segments on its rattle. The body was supposedly as thick as a nail keg. The report is noted in Michael Newton's *Giant Snakes: Unraveling the Coils of Mystery*, though no further details are provided.

Cryptozoologist Loren Coleman related a giant snake tale from Utah on the *Cryptomundo* blog. The February 6, 2010, posting reported that the account was sent in to *Cryptomundo* and involved an elderly Paiute woman and a male friend from Price, Utah, who were chasing down a family legend. The article reports:

"The lady's grandfather had said there was an underground city, and gold mines, under the Henry Mountains in Utah, near the former site of what the grandfather described as the 'Serpent Temple.' The grandfather had a hand drawn picture of the entrance to the temple—showing giant snakes carved in rock. He claimed the picture was from his family and the temple had been destroyed and buried to hide the site."

During their search for the lost mine, the man claims to have witnessed a giant snake, one 35 feet in length. The man reports that he was observing some cattle at a spring near the site when the serpent appeared and struck. The snake took down a one-year-old calf that weighed at least 150 pounds. The report continues:

"He estimated the snake to be over 35ft in length. He claimed it knocked the calf over and quickly wrapped around it and he watched fascinated and terrified as it took a rather long period of time to engulf the calf."

But the account doesn't end with this incident. Reportedly, the same man, and his female friend, claimed to have seen the monstrous serpents on numerous occasions. The man spoke to a local rancher to find out if he was missing cattle. The rancher reported that "rustlers" were stealing 10 to 12 cows a year from his ranch.

Even more dramatic, the woman claimed to have come face to face with one of the snakes. She was sitting on a rock by a dirt road in the area when one of the serpents came out, rose up to the height of her face, and stared at her. The snake opened its mouth, and the woman says the odor from the thing's breath was quite foul.

The woman had routinely caught, and eaten, snakes in her youth, but says that the giant she saw that day was unlike any other snake she had ever encountered. The *Cryptomundo* report continues:

"She described its skin as leathery, rather than having the scales she was used to seeing. Furthermore, its head ('bigger than my head'), had some kind of dorsal ridge down it. After a long moment, it lowered its head and crossed the road at a diagonal, disappearing down the hill on the other side. The tail was apparently on one side of the road as the head reached the other. The lady and the guy claimed to have measured the distance at well over 28ft."

The story is certainly incredible, but is there any truth to it? Outside of a few stories, there's no evidence for the existence of such giants in the Utah mountains.

It is notable, however, that there are some interesting folkloric connections to giant snakes in the area.

The Henry Mountains are in the southeastern portion of the state and run in a general north-south direction for about thirty miles. The region was once Southern Paiute territory. Curiously, the Southern Paiutes and related Northern Paiute, Bannock, and Shoshone tribes were once known collectively as "Snake Indians." The term was used as early as 1739 by French Canadian trader and explorer Pierre Gaultier de Varennes, sieur de La Vérendrye who likely heard about the "Snake people" from either the Lakota or the Mandan tribe.

Determining the origin of why the tribes were referred to as Snake people is difficult. The term may have come about by simple accident with a mispronunciation of a native word, or the origin could be more complex. Either way, the term stuck for a long time and early pioneers commonly referred to several tribes in the area as Snake people.

As for the Henry Mountains, there's plenty of interesting tales associated with the range. In the late 1700s, the Spanish mined for gold in the mountains, convinced there was a motherlode in the range. The Spanish captured local natives and forced them into backbreaking labor in the mines. For years, the Spanish hauled gold out of the mountains. Tired of their suffering and enslavement, the natives rebelled and killed the Spanish invaders. After the battle, the mine entrances were destroyed, packed with rocks, and hidden. To further ensure no one else would come after the gold, a curse was placed on the area.

Historian Edward T. Wolverton wrote about the cursed mine in his 1928 manuscript *Legends, Traditions and Early History of the Henry Mountains*. According to Wolverton:

"To him who reopened the mines some great calamity will come. His blood will turn to water, and even in youth he will be as an old man...various other punishments will attend to him; too numerous to mention."

Wolverton doesn't mention giant snakes, but his notes on the curse and the gravity with which it was long viewed gives us an indication of just how many strange stories and superstitions surround the mountains.

Additionally, it's interesting to note that the Paiutes claimed the snakes were put in the area in part to protect the site and keep people away from the gold.

Tales of hidden tunnels and lost mines can be found all over the state. Sometimes the accounts involve serpent guardians or giant snakes who have taken up residence in the caves and tunnels.

One curious tale that I've heard several times involves a hidden tunnel near Alpine in Utah County. Reportedly, an area farmer asked for help moving a large boulder out of his field so that he could plant his crops. A group of men came to his aid and when the boulder was moved, the entrance to an underground tunnel was revealed. The men ventured inside only to discover a giant snake blocking their path. They managed to escape back to the surface where they pushed the boulder back in place to seal the snake inside.

Giant snakes have been reported around the San Juan River

Several people have recounted the story to me over the years, but no one seemed to know the original source of the account. The *Utah UFO Hunters* website has a small paragraph about the incident and credits a man named John Hall and the *Conspiracy Archive* website. However, the thread has been removed from that site so it's difficult to follow up on.

My Crypto Four Corners colleague, the late JC Johnson, pursued some giant snake reports that he received from the southeastern portion of the state around the San Juan River.

JC collected numerous accounts and found notable reports from 2005 and 2007. He interviewed witnesses who had spotted large water snakes on the river, with one stunning report from a man who said the creature he saw was approximately thirty feet in length.

Johnson investigated the locations of the reports himself and found what he believed was evidence to support the possibility of unusual sized snakes in the San Juan. Johnson described a snake, 10" to 12" in diameter that left the water, went onto the river's bank, and slithered its way to his parked truck where it briefly reared up to the vehicle's back bumper.

JC further noted that the snake was dark in color with markings similar to those of an Indian/Burmese python or a species of anaconda. Johnson speculated that such an exotic species could explain sightings in the area. Of course, this in and of itself is a mystery. Neither pythons nor anacondas are native to Utah. If people were indeed seeing such an out-of-place snake, there are a couple of possible explanations.

The snakes might be the result of an exotic pet owner turning them loose in the wild to let them fend for themselves. This is known to happen with exotic species when they become too large or too unmanageable for the owners.

Other people have suggested the presence of an invasive species, but there's no indication that this is the case in Utah. The state's climate makes it unlikely that an exotic constrictor could survive in the wild long term.

If the thought of potential large, invasive constrictors or ancient giant snakes from a lost temple aren't creepy enough for you, what about a giant, flying snake?

Writing on the *Mysterious Universe* website, Brent Swancer reports a bizarre incident from May 2005.

According to Swancer, a witness and two friends were in the Salt Lake City area when they spotted a strange creature that was "in tall grass feeding on the carcass of a dead deer."

The thing was described as nine feet in length with an estimated weight of about 245 pounds. The creature was dark brown in color and had purple stripes, glowing eyes, and small wings on its back.

The unidentified witness also reported a scar that was visible between the animal's eyes and a rancid stench coming from the beast that was like that of a "dead skunk and sewer." Swancer reports:

"The witness said he observed the snake feeding for several minutes from about 4 yards away before it noticed his presence, after which it hissed and raced away into the grass at great speed."

One wonders why the thing didn't go airborne, but perhaps the tiny wings weren't functional.

A report dated August 2000 was posted on Ghost Source. com under their "True Encounters Archive."

The reporting witness was having a BBQ when the sky suddenly went pitch black. Those gathered for the event looked up and saw "several skinny, bony, black creatures with wings flying at a rapid pace over the city."

The same report states that another witness was parked in her driveway and saw something similar. She described the creatures as "five weird, skinny, black creatures with round, big eyes."

The creatures were apparently aggressive, broke the car window to get at the woman, and bit her on the arm.

She reported the incident and police officers told her that she had been attacked by a pack of dogs.

There's a problem with this entire report right from the start—the events purportedly took place in Colchester, Utah, yet no such place seems to exist. A search of cities and towns in the state, including variations, doesn't even yield anything close to such a place.

I have included the account in this volume because I've seen it on various listings of cryptid encounters in the state. Until or unless a clarification of the location surfaces, or one of the actual witnesses comes forward, we must discard it as a possible fabrication.

Weird Humanoids

Dry Fork Canyon is an unusual area with a dark history. Over the years, strange occurrences have been reported in the canyon.

One frequently repeated incident involves a pair of suicides that occurred six months apart. Both were men, and both did something very strange prior to jumping to their deaths. They undressed, folded their clothing in a neat stack, then leapt off the cliff.

Authorities were puzzled by the cases and discovered that both men had, at different times, dated the same woman. No evidence of foul play was found but investigators were left scratching their heads over the strange aspects of the deaths.

Some people think the cause of the men's strange behavior was the location itself. Dry Fork Canyon is said to be a very strange place. Some think it's cursed or haunted, others believe it's the abode of strange creatures.

An article by Stephen Wagner on the now defunct Paranormal About website detailed a case of bizarre creatures in Dry Fork Canyon.

The reporting witness, listed as Gus B., said that his encounters in the canyon took place in May 2003 when he and his brother attended a wedding reception being held in Maine Park (This area is officially Remember the Maine Park) just outside of Vernal in Uintah County.

After enjoying the reception for a time, the witness and four others decided to take a trek out into the woods to do some exploring. One member of the group noted that the area was known for strange events, but this didn't deter the men from their expedition.

They left around five o'clock and after about fifteen minutes of walking, they noticed that the temperature had dropped. The reporting witness says that he started to feel unsettled at this point.

As they continued walking, they came to a spot where, for about a hundred yards, the ground was covered with the bones of cattle. The sight was a bit unsettling, but the men continued their trek. A little further on, the hikers came to an area of thick trees. The man's brother tapped him and quietly asked if he saw what was nearby. He recalls:

"About fifteen yards away in the thick woods was a distinguishable, dark shape that was *huge*. It looked like a gorilla sitting on its knuckles, but it was completely black, and far too tall to be a bear, as it was about seven feet tall in this crouching position!"

The rest of the group took notice of the figure, and they all continued their walk in a different direction. After a few moments, the witness's younger brother wanted to go back to the wedding party, so he and another member of the group set off to return to the reception.

The hikers continued into the woods and soon experienced strange noises, "hooting" sounds that came out of nowhere and red eyes flashing in the growing darkness. Things soon became more intense with the appearance of weird humanoid figures. The witness states:

"I turned around to see a good number of grayish-white humanoid figures running, blinking, and just basically freaking out. The thing that got me running is that they were rapidly heading our way!"

The group fled the area and raced back to the park where the reception was still going on. They were shocked to learn that they had been gone for six hours.

Whatever the men had experienced, it was enough to keep them from ever going back into the canyon.

In his book *The Inhumanoids*, Barton Nunnelly reports a weird creature sighting from Huntsville in Weber County.

On the evening of June 13, 2005, at around 1:30 a.m., a couple were having a quiet moment at Cemetery Point when they were shocked by the appearance of a weird, squat humanoid creature walking on two legs.

The thing was described as "about 3' 6" with a hairy body, reptilian facial features and noticeable protruding nipples."

At first, the creature was walking upright but it seemed to be hunchbacked. When it realized it was being observed, it froze for a moment and made a "loud gagging sound." It then dropped down on all fours and ran away.

According to the witness, the creature moved like a deer and reached an estimated speed of thirty mph as it fled the scene. It quickly disappeared in the darkness.

The witness reported that there was a strong smell of bleach that seemed to come from the creature.

Prehistoric Survivors

Camelops was a genus of large North American camel-like animals with long necks, long legs, and most likely a single hump. They were thought to have died out around 10,000 years ago, but this theory was called into question in 1926 when an unusual skull discovery was made in Fillmore, Utah.

Albert S. Romer examined the find and wrote about it in the July 6, 1928, edition of *Science* under the headline "A 'Fossil' Camel Recently Living in Utah." Romer reports:

"It [the skull] consists of a practically complete braincase and most of the palate. The bone is perfectly fresh in appearance; no replacement had occurred; a bit of dried muscle is still present on the basioccipital."

Romer's careful investigation of the skull showed that it was not from a modern camel and that it matched the prehistoric creature in question. The article also reported on the conditions of the find:

"The specimen was discovered by two high-school boys of Fillmore, Utah, who, at the time, were exploring the igneous buttes some twenty miles south and west of that village. It was found about two hundred feet back in a cave, buried under about three or four feet of fine dry eolian deposit, which was easy to excavate. The cave is one of many caverns formed in the old lava beds of the district."

Some scientists were of the opinion that the skull had been well preserved because it was buried in a layer of fine dust three to four feet thick. Even if this were the case, the find indicated that the creatures likely lived in the region later than was previously assumed.

It is, at the least, interesting when considered with the

fact that there are folkloric and Native American mentions of camels, or camel-like creatures roaming around Utah in earlier times.

Another ancient creature that likely lived in the region much longer than is commonly believed is the Mammoth.

In Moab, there's a petroglyph known as the "Moab Mammoth," or the "Moab Mastodon."

The October 1935 issue of *The Scientific Monthly* mentions the image in a brief article titled "The Moab Mastodon Pictograph."

The ancient image is between two and three feet in length. Some believe it shows a mammoth, or mastodon, with a its trunk, tusks, and elephant-like feet visible. One interpretation is that the animal is using its trunk to spray its back with water.

Another petroglyph near the Butler Wash-San Juan River confluence area also shows what many interpret as a mammoth or mastodon.

The possibility of such creatures surviving beyond the commonly accepted timeframe doesn't sit well with many officials who go out of their way to explain the anomalies. My friend David West once heard an expert offer his explanation for the mammoth pictograph. West recalls the "expert's" explanation:

"He postulated that of course there never were any mammoths in Utah and that this was the case of a dude who travelled all the way from Alaska just to draw them on an island in Utah. It beggars belief but that's the academic answer—it's even more ridiculous than just accepting that mammoths were present in Utah much later than is the accepted time frame."

Another pictograph discovered in a Utah canyon implies that natives in the area were aware of flying giants.

The pictograph is in Black Dragon Canyon, fifteen miles west of Green River. In 1928, rock art was discovered that appears to depict a bird seven feet long with massive, batlike wings, a tail, and a head crest—at least—that has long been the common assumption. Findings in recent years seem to indicate a different answer.

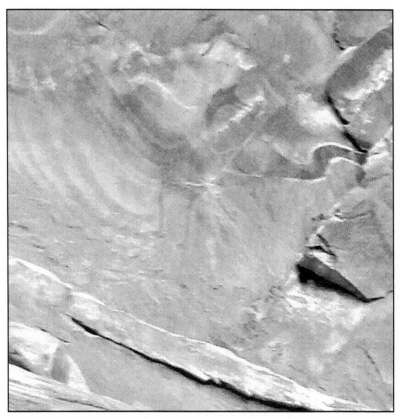

The pictograph at Black Dragon Canyon

The art was determined to have been painted by members of the Fremont culture who lived in the area between A.D. 900-1100.

According to an article published in 2015 in Volume 89 of the journal *Antiquity*, the red pigment art isn't a singular figure at all. Under the banner "The Death of a Pterodactyl," researchers reported findings discovered by using cutting-edge techniques to examine the art. Portable X-ray fluorescence equipment revealed that the art consists of five separate images including a sheep, a dog, a small figure, a tall figure, and a serpent-like figure. Paul Bahn, freelance archeologist, and co-lead of the research project, noted:

"It is not a single figure. It is not a pterodactyl. It's a beautiful set of images."

It's interesting to note that little has been said about the new images containing a "serpent-like figure." Giant snakes anyone?

For some, the news is no doubt disappointing, but the findings certainly aren't the final word on the topic of native Americans and giant, winged creatures and many people still believe that the Black Dragon image is what it looks like—a giant, prehistoric flying creature.

One woman who visited the site told me she believes the ancient people who painted the image intentionally layered several other images to create the winged beast.

Evidence of prehistoric creatures that lived a bit beyond the accepted time range is one thing, but what if there were still dinosaurs roaming the Utah deserts? Some witnesses swear that's exactly what they've seen.

Reportedly, small herds of fast moving, two legged creatures have been spotted around southern Utah. The beasts reportedly resemble a miniature "allosaurus" or miniature T. Rex and move quickly across the landscape on two legs.

JC Johnson and I spoke to a witness who claimed that three of the creatures ran in front of his vehicle in late summer 2003. The man said he was driving outside of Moab one afternoon when he saw something moving off the road on the right-hand side of the roadway. He slowed down and finally came to a complete stop as the creatures, one by one, ran across the blacktop. He said they were around three feet in height and ran on two legs.

"I swear they were small dinosaurs, just like out of Jurassic Park. I've never seen anything like that before or since. I know it sounds crazy, but I know what I saw."

A different witness told Johnson and me that he'd seen a similar creature in the Arches National Park. The man said he was hiking with his uncle, and they had stopped to drink some water and enjoy the scenery. Perched on some high rocks, the pair looked at the landscape around them. They were at a high point and could seen a flat area well below them. A creature came out from behind some rocks to the far left and ran across the flat area. The men watched it, puzzled by the strange appearance. A second creature appeared running behind the first and the two darted across the landscape kicking up a trail of dust as they did so. They soon vanished behind a hill.

"There's no doubt in my mind, that those things were dinosaurs. They looked like small T. Rexes!"

Strange things have been reported
around Arches National Park

Johnson told me he'd heard several similar reports over the years and that they all came from the deserts of southern Utah with the Canyonlands and Arches National Parks being the focal points of the sightings.

A man named Leonard emailed me about a creature he spotted in 2012. The incident occurred on a dirt road outside of Moab.

Leonard and his girlfriend were out for a drive around sunset. They were in "an intense conversation" and Leonard, who was driving, kept glancing over at his girlfriend. He recounts:

"I was looking at my girl and I saw something move in front of the truck, so I hit the brakes quick and looked out in front of me. I hadn't hit it and this thing was running off to my right by that time, but a second one was behind it, it was a freaking dinosaur, like a little T. Rex kind of thing running on two legs. Brown and leathery looking with a big head."

The late JC Johnson (left) and the author in the field

A truck driver hauling a semi-truck loaded with potatoes saw what he believed was a prehistoric big cat in 1987.

The man was traveling on Interstate 80 headed east toward the Wyoming border. The trucker's routine drive was interrupted when he spotted a big cat on the side of the road. It was tan colored and appeared to be stalking something. The man slowed the truck down to get a better look at the animal and quickly realized that it was something unusual. He described the creature in a report filed with *Utah UFO Hunters*:

"This big tan-looking cat was very muscular and I mean very muscular, more so than a puma or mountain lion would be. You could see all of the muscles bulging out everywhere on its body and face when it walked and ran. And this cat had a very short, stubby tail. To me this cat resembled the large cat family that you would see normally in a museum or history books, as a saber-tooth tiger or lion."

So, what are we to make of such reports? Misidentification? Desert mirages? The potential of living survivors from prehistoric ages is difficult for many to accept, even those interested in cryptozoology, but unless we assume that all of the reports are fake, then there's no easy way to explain what witnesses are seeing.

The deserts of the American Southwest are certainly mysterious and perhaps they have more secrets yet to be revealed.

BEEHIVE STATE MONSTERS by David Weatherly

Acknowledgements

Special thanks to my friend David West for the great foreword and his input on Utah legends.

I continue to be grateful for the support and input of my friends and colleagues as this series continues to progress, including Loren Coleman, Dr. Jeff Meldrum, Christopher O'Brien, John LeMay, Jay Bachochin, Lyle Blackburn, Chad Lewis, Kevin Nelson, and Nick Redfern.

Thanks to Mister Sam Shearon for yet another fantastic cover for the series, Eddie at SMAK Graphics for layout and Jerry Hajewski for editing.

Last but not least, thanks to the many witnesses and organizations who have shared their sightings, opinions and information.

Bibliography

Behle, Dr. William H., Cottam, Dr. W.P. Further Light on the 'Fossil' Bird Nests of the Great Salt Lake Desert. University of Utah. 1943.

Bell, Lee D. South Weber: The Autobiography of One Utah Community. Self-published, Salt Lake City, UT. 1990.

Bowman, Matthew. A Mormon Bigfoot: David Patten's Cain and the Conception of Evil in LDS Folklore. Journal of Mormon History, Fall 2007 (Vol.33 No. 3).

Coleman, Loren and Huyghe, Patrick. The Field Guide to Lake Monsters, Sea Serpents, and other Mystery Denizens of the Deep. Tarcher/Penguin, New York, NY. 2003.

Crowe, Ray. Bigfoot Behavior Volume II. CreateSpace Independent Publishing, Scotts Valley, CA. 2015.

Dunning, Linda. Lost Landscapes: Utah's Ghosts, Mysterious Creatures, and Aliens. Council Press, Springville, UT. 2007.

Godfrey, Linda. I Know What I Saw: Modern-Day Encounters with Monsters of New Urban Legend and Ancient Lore. TarcherPerigee, New York, NY. 2020.

Jameson, W.C. Unsolved Mysteries of the Old West. Taylor Trade Publishing, Fort Worth, TX. 1999.

Kelleher, Colm A. and Knapp, George. Hunt for the Skinwalker Science Confronts the Unexplained at a Remote Ranch in Utah. Paraview Pocket Books, New York, NY. 2005.

Kimball, Spencer. The Miracle of Forgiveness. Bookcraft Publishing, Salt Lake City, UT. 1969.

Lester, Shane. Clan of Cain: The Genesis of Bigfoot. Booklocker Publishing, Saint Petersburg, FL. 2001.

Martineau, LaVan. Southern Paiutes Legend, Lore, Language and Lineage. KC Publications, Las Vegas, NV. 1992.

Newton, Michael. Giant Snakes: Unraveling the Coils of Mystery. CFZ Press, Bideford, North Devon, England. 2009.

Nunnelly, Barton. The Inhumanoids. CFZ Press, Bideford, North Devon, England. 2011.

O'Brien, Christopher. Stalking the Tricksters, Shapeshifters, Skinwalkers, Dark Adepts and 2012. Adventures Unlimited Press, Kempton, IL, 2009.

Rich, Russell R. Land of the Sky-Blue Water: A History of the LDS Settlement in Bear Lake Valley. Bear Lake Publishing, Montpelier, UT. Second Edition 2001.

Rife, Philip. Bigfoot Across America. Writers Club Press, Lincoln, NE 2000.

Robinson, Phil. Sinners and Saints: Three Months Among the Mormons. LDS Church, Salt Lake City, UT. 1883.

Ross, Kerry and Boren, Lisa Lee. The Gold of the Carre-Shinob. Bonneville Books, Springville, UT. 1998.

Smith, Anne M. Ute Tales. University of Utah Press, Salt Lake City, UT. 1992.

Strickler, Lon. Phantoms and Monsters: Mysterious Encounters. Triangulum Publishing, Boulder, CO. 2016.

Thatcher, Elaine. Between Pulpit and Pew: The Supernatural World in Mormon History and Folklore. Utah State University Press, Logan, UT. 2011.

Thompson, Bonnie. Folklore in the Bear Lake Valley. Granite Publishing Company, Salt Lake City, UT. 1972.

Weeks, Andy. Haunted Utah Ghosts and Strange Phenomena of the Beehive State. Stackpole Books, Mechanicsburg, PA. 2012.

Wolverton, Edward T. Legends, Traditions, and Early History of the Henry Mountains. Utah State Historical Society manuscript collection, Salt Lake City, UT. 1928.

Magazines & Journals

Antiquity.

Frontier Times, Winter 1960.

Journal of Vertebrate Paleontology Volume 25 Issue 4.

Science July 1928.

Scientific Monthly October 1935.

True Frontier.

Utah Stories Magazine.

Online Resources

BFRO (Bigfoot Field Researchers Organization)

Bigfoot Encounters

Bigfoot Seekers

Cryptomundo

Earthfiles

Gaia

Hunt the Skinwalker

Mysterious Universe

Oregonbigfoot.com

Sasq-Wasatch

Skinwalker Ranch

Utah Bigfoot Blog

Utah Bigfoot Files

Utah UFO Hunters

Photo Credits

Black Dragon Canyon photo by David West.

Oquirrh Mountains photo by Don LaVange via Creative Commons. Creative Commons — Attribution-ShareAlike 2.0 Generic — CC BY-SA 2.0

All other photos by David Weatherly or are held in the public domain.

Bibliography

About the Author

David Weatherly

David Weatherly is a renaissance man of the strange and supernatural. He has traveled the world in pursuit of ghosts, cryptids, UFOs, magic, and more. From the specters of dusty castles, to remote, haunted islands, from ancient sites, to modern mysteries, he has journeyed to the most unusual places on the globe seeking the unknown.

David became fascinated with the paranormal at a young age. Ghost stories and accounts of weird creatures and UFOs led him to discover many of his early influences. Writers such as John Keel, Jacques Vallee, Hans Holzer, and others set him on course to spend his life exploring and investigating the unexplained.

Throughout his life, he's also delved into shamanic and magical traditions from around the world, spending time with elders from numerous cultures in Europe, the Americas, Africa, and Asia. He has studied with Taoist masters in China, Tibetan Lamas, and other mystics from the far east. He's picked up knowledge from African and Native American tribal elders and sat around fires with shamans from countless other traditions.

Along his path, David has also gathered a lot of arcane knowledge, studying a range of ancient arts from palmistry, the runes, and other obscure forms of divination, to alchemy and magick. He has studied and taught Qigong and Ninjutsu, as well as various energy related arts. David has also studied stage and performance magic.

His shamanic and magical background has given him a unique perspective in his explorations into the unknown, and he continues to write, travel, and explore, leaving no stone unturned in his quest for the strange and unusual.

David has investigated, and written about, a diverse range of topics, including, Hauntings & Ghosts, Cryptozoology, Ufology, Ancient Mysteries, Shamanism, Magic, and Psychic Phenomena.

David is the founder of the independent media and publishing company, Eerie Lights Publishing.

He has been a featured speaker at conferences around the world and has lectured for countless paranormal and spiritual groups.

He is a frequent guest on *Coast to Coast AM* with George Noory, *Spaced Out Radio* and other radio programs. David has also appeared on numerous television shows including the Travel Channel's *Mysteries of the Outdoors*, History Channel's *Ancient Aliens, Beyond Belief* and other programs. He was also featured in the highly successful series *On the Trail of UFOs*.

David's books include *Strange Intruders, Eerie Companions,* the Monsters of America series, and the *Haunted* series.

Find David online at:

https://eerielights.com

Made in the USA
Las Vegas, NV
15 August 2023

76156268R00148